Alsace-Lorraine
by
George Wharton Edwards

*"Open my heart and you will see
The land all emblazoned with Fleurs des Lys."*

Windham Press is committed to bringing the lost cultural heritage of ages past into the 21st century through high-quality reproductions of original, classic printed works at affordable prices.

This book has been carefully crafted to utilize the original images of antique books rather than error-prone OCR text. This also preserves the work of the original typesetters of these classics, unknown craftsmen who laid out the text, often by hand, of each and every page you will read. Their subtle art involving judgment and interaction with the text is in many ways superior and more human than the mechanical methods utilized today, and gave each book a unique, hand-crafted feel in its text that connected the reader organically to the art of bindery and book-making.

We think these benefits are worth the occasional imperfection resulting from the age of these books at the time of scanning, and their vintage feel provides a connection to the past that goes beyond the mere words of the text.

As bibliophiles, we are always seeking perfection in our work, so please notify us of any errors in this book by emailing us at corrections@windhampress.com. Our team is motivated to correct errors quickly so future customers are better served. Our mission is to raise the bar of quality for reprinted works by a focus on detail and quality over mass production.

To peruse our catalog of carefully curated classic works, please visit our online store at www.windhampress.com.

WINDHAM PRESS
CLASSIC REPRINTS

'A childhood land of mountain ways,
Where earthly gnomes and forest fays,
Kind foolish giants, gentle bears,
Sport with the peasant as he fares
Affrighted through the forest glades,
And lead sweet wistful little maids
Lost in the woods, forlorn, alone,
To princely lovers and a throne.

.   .   .   .

Dear haunted land of gorge and glen,
Ah, me! the dreams, the dreams of men!

A learned land of wise old books
'And men with meditative looks,
Who move in quaint red-gabled towns
And sit in gravely folded gowns,
Divining in deep-laden speech
The world's supreme arcana—each
A homely god to listening Youth
Eager to tear the veil of Truth;

.   .   .   .

Mild votaries of book and pen—
Alas, the dreams, the dreams of men!

'A music land, whose life is wrought
In movement of melodious thought;
In symphony, great wave on wave—
Or fugue, elusive, swift, and grave;
A singing land, whose lyric rimes
Float on the air like village chimes;
Music and verse—the deepest part
Of a whole nation's thinking heart!

.   .   .   .

Oh, land of Now, oh, land of Then!
Dear God! the dreams, the dreams of men!

Ōh, depths beneath sweet human ken,
God help the dreams, the dreams of men!

ANON.

From *London Punch*, 1917.

To
My Beloved Lady Anne

Foreword

THE one dominating purpose of the people of Alsace-Lorraine is their reunion with the mother country: France. A temporary or final autonomy for the Lost Provinces, this "Land of Unshed Tears," is out of the question. The people do not want it. It would be most impracticable to establish it. They would not even discuss it. The people of Alsace-Lorraine consider themselves French and a part of France.

The creation of even a temporary autonomy would be nothing more than a makeshift, a deferring of the whole question, and history shows conclusively that there is no attempted settlement so dangerous to ultimate peace as such a makeshift; a temporary autonomy such as Germany proposes. The only logical way to settle the matter is to sever completely the enforced, undesired and unnatural connection between the provinces and Germany, and return them, with as good grace as they can assume, to their natural place as part of France.

There is no way of causing the self-expatriated inhabitants of Alsace-Lorraine, who fled rather than live under the Prussian rule, to return to it under an autonomy.

FOREWORD

In the United States, in England, and in France, there are half a million of Alsatians who would not consent to leave their adopted homes and new occupations for the doubtful opportunity of taking part in a plebiscite in the country of their birth. They know too well the touch of the iron hand.

The seizure in 1871 of Alsace-Lorraine is regarded by the Germans as the crowning triumph and victory of the Bismarckian era of conquest, and it must be made for them by ourselves and our Allies one of the reasons for their defeat in the present war, which that blood-steeped war master of Europe has precipitated upon the nations for their domination.

The wrong done to Belgium is not greater than that done to Alsace-Lorraine, save that the latter country has not yet been so wrecked by fire and sword.

How can the wrong to either nation be righted save by restoration?

How else than by France's recovery of the provinces so wrongfully seized, can Germany be defeated?— Treaties with a government which contemptuously regards them as "scraps of paper" is play for children or Bolsheviki.

Indemnity without a return of such territory is not to be considered. Germany must not merely be made to give up what she has seized; she must lose as well the material resources upon which her iniquitous enterprise was based.

In 1871 no plebiscite was taken, although both France and Alsace-Lorraine vainly urged it. Why, then, should there be one now, or at a period after the end of the present war? "Has there not even been a continuous plebiscite in Alsace-Lorraine from the protests of the elected representatives of these provinces at the National Assembly in Bordeaux in 1871 and in the Reichstag in Berlin in 1874, and on up to the popular protests of Savern (Zabern) in 1913?" (Clement Rueff.)

The possibility of even a fair competition between Germany and France to an autonomous Alsace-Lorraine is unbelievable. After what has happened to Belgium and other countries no one can believe in such a suggestion. It must be *won* upon the battlefield where France stands an even chance, at least. Germany can be intimidated or won over only by a show of force. She cannot comprehend gentler methods. A people who glory in such acts as the sinking of the *Lusitania;* the murder of Edith Cavell, and Captain Fryatt; the placing of young children and their mothers before the marching soldiers; the assault upon undefended towns; the bombing of hospitals; the slavery of French and Belgian women. Those who applaud the acts of Von Bernstorff and Luxburg, would hardly stop at similar methods in their deal-

ings with Alsace-Lorraine if they thought necessary.
France would perish before using such means to subju-
gate.

Concerning the treatment of Germans in the provinces
when they are eventually returned to France, witness how
France treated Alsace in 1648 after it became French.

Both Protestants and Jews were baited and persecuted
in Paris and throughout France, yet in Alsace they were
tolerated, even protected from interference, and allowed
to worship according to their peculiar tenets.

"The very question of language, which has so often
been raised by Germany to prove that Alsace is German,
is it not a conclusive demonstration of the extreme tolerance of France? If France had used the same methods
that Germany has used since 1871, can one think for a
moment that the Alsatian dialect could have remained
the popular language of Alsace after 200 years of French
occupation? And let us not forget that an appreciable
part of Alsace, with such towns as Thann, St. Amarin,
Massevaux, Dannemarie, has been occupied by France
since 1914 and has been incorporated with that other
part of the Department of the Haut-Rhin, Belfort and
surroundings, which remained a part of France after
1871.

"The French Government since 1914 has not ceased to
give this question of the period of transition the most

FOREWORD

earnest thought, and to this effect a special and official commission has been created, composed of prominent Alsatians and Lorrainers of all standings, with the purpose of studying this question from all points of view and of elaborating the means of preventing all friction with the people of Alsace-Lorraine regarding their religious, political and economical relations after their reunion with France.

"And I can find no better demonstration as to what will be the attitude of the mother country toward her recovered children than by repeating the words of the great and good Joffre to the people of Thann when he first came to that old Alsatian city; words that made the tears rise to the eyes of all old Alsatians who heard him, and that still make the tears rise to mine, when he said: "Je vous apporte le baiser de la France." (Clement Rueff).[1]

And so that the reader may know just what sort of people are these Alsace-Lorrainers—how some of them live, and under what conditions—I have gathered these random notes together, and ransacked my sketch books for types of people, and pictures of the old castles in the mountainous districts; the nestling small towns in the thick forests; the great rivers flowing through lovely meadow lands lined with marvelous old towns and villages, which transport one who tarries there into the mid-

[1] V. P. Association Générale des Alsaciens-Lorraine d' Amérique.

FOREWORD

dle age. Then there is such a wealth of mediæval churches and abbeys, ruined turreted castles glorified in legend, and exquisite old châteaux embowered in the shade of great trees. . . . And so, dear reader, may it charm you as it has the author.

Greenwich, Conn.,
    May 22, 1918.

Contents

List of Illustrations

LIST OF ILLUSTRATIONS

The Lost Provinces

The Lost Provinces

WHEN we get to the top of the road, M'sieur, we shall be in Alsace. There is a post there to mark the boundary—the frontier—*'bien entendu.'* On this side one sees the shield of France, but, *'toute au coup,'* once one has passed, one sees that it bears the black *'bête'* of Germany on the other side, and then one is in Alsace!"

Thus the driver of our auto, not really our own, but one that we had hired for the day at Belfort for the thirty odd mile drive to Mulhouse. Through this green-gold hay-and-honeysuckle-breathing afternoon the low valley welcomes us along perfect roads to the boundary. Occasionally drowsy laborers, despite Sunday, are loitering in the fields; we pass two huge cream colored oxen hitched to an immense hay cart, a peasant lolling in a doze high on the fragrant hay—a small white stoned cemetery with the majestic Crucified Figure above a blazing labyrinth of hollyhock and sunflower; then a village of some score or more of creamy-walled homes topped by a gray old spire. Then a fringe of purplish gray poplars, sentinel-like, on either hand. The wooded heights grow into mountains all crested with ancient gray ruin of historical strongholds. The Dukes of Lorraine coveted these; took by force, and sometimes married them with their Chatelaines. Louis XIV likewise coveted them, and ravaged them with fire and blood by the iron hand of Boufflers. The Barons were given little or no notice of his coming; the family might be at breakfast over the second cup of whatever it was they used instead of coffee, or the sleepy sentinel on the tower might be aroused by the clatter of approaching cavaliers and cannon along the winding road. Cannon and powder brought the doom of the great strongholds so long deemed impregnable. The massive towers fell like ninepins under the blast, and many vanished into dust, leaving hardly a trace to mark the site now so exquisitely draped in ivy. Thus the whole region became what the tourist calls "picturesque."

THE LOST PROVINCES

No two agree as to just what constitutes a state of picturesqueness, but perhaps dilapidation forms an essential part of it. Certainly these ruins are as dilapidated as one could wish, and this warrior Boufflers was the cause of it.

The unfortunate peasants of the region, who then eked out wretched existences, as it were, between hammer and anvil, chased hither and yon by the marauders, dodging the bolts and the chance morsels of bastion or tower that flew about during these busy days when Boufflers demolished their humble homes, have made way for a posterity that now enjoys jingling the freely given francs of the appreciative tourist. Everywhere there was this day a look of smiling contentment; little gardens where are flowing brooks, and buff or heliotrope colored cottage walls, with windows bright with fuchsias, roses and dahlias, and here and there the flower framed face of a woman glancing out at us as we passed. "V'la, les Touristes."—They have come! The sun shining with spendthrift glory flooded the long smooth road and the low houses.

The eye passed over nests of sweet clover; over the tops of apple and peach trees now frosted with blossoms. The fields were full of cattle, and the women who watched them ceaselessly knitted. They were broad hipped figures clad in coarse skirts of blue or brown stuff, with dark bodices and bright pink or orange kerchiefs.

Some of these toiled from the fields bearing full jugs of milk, which they carried not ungracefully. In the distance were the figures of ploughmen, rising and falling with the rolling of the land, turning the fertile sod for the new crop. All was peaceful on the Alsatian border that sunny afternoon of 1910.

"At the top of the road, M'sieur and Madame, just above, is the boundary line between France and Alsace," said the chauffeur. "On this side you will see a monument, on the top of which is a cock in bronze looking towards France. Below, M'sieur and Madame will see a bronze figure of Victory with wreaths in each hand, and on the stone shaft is carved the words, 'To the Soldiers of France, who died for their Country.' There fell my father in 1870. Always there are wreaths of fresh flowers on the mounds hereabouts, but those who lay them there are mainly the children of exiles from German Alsace now living in France."

Here lies the frontier, its boundary marked by the tall iron pole, striped with black and white, and bearing on a shield at the top, on one side the arms of France with the letters R. F. and on the reverse, the sprawled out and crowned eagle of Prussia, over which are the words "*Deutsches Reich*," the mark of the Usurper, the oppressor, which the children of the country-side call "La Chauve-Souris" (The Bat)—not aloud, you understand, but in half whispers among themselves. Upon the occasion of my first visit, twenty years after the Franco-Prussian war, such frankness was inadvisable on the border. Crossing the Vosges at that time into Alsace-Lorraine, it was then difficult for the tourist to "get at" the people; they were still too sore at heart to talk much even if they trusted one,—and the painter is ever trusted by the peasants, and cordially welcomed to the house and a place at the fireside freely offered to him. At these firesides one has sat quietly listening to the discussions of the elders, who at times forgot the presence of the stranger, and voiced their feelings freely. One has thus listened to their opinions of the annexation; of the Protestation of 1874 at Strassburg and Mulhouse; of the agitations of 1887; of the dissolution of the Reichstag; of the Boulangist movement in Paris; the Schnaebele incident, and the passport regulations, down to the Zabern outrage. But even after this intimacy it is not proper to say that one knows the people, so that these notes must not be taken in a more serious vein than that in which they are written, the object being perhaps to entertain rather than to instruct. The route followed is haphazard, and this book is quite useless as a guide book. With this warning the reader may be content to proceed.

One may well pardon the Alsatians for saying and believing that their country is the most beautiful on earth, for it offers to the eye a panorama of exquisite hill and valley and silvery streams. Lying between the Vosges and the Jura and bordered by the curve of the Rhine lies this little country, the land of unshed tears. Mulhouse is at the entrance or foyer, Belfort (Vosges) at one side and Huningue (Jura) at the other. The railway parallels the Rhine from Wissembourg-Hagenau to Strassburg, branching off to Schlestadt-Ribeauville and returning to Mulhouse. The whole length of the Vosges one sees the evidences of the ancient torrents, in the sandy plateaus and the talus left by the glaciers.

The mountains and high hills are crowned by heavy forests of oak and pine, in which are yet found the ancient altars of the Druids, and dotted here and there with the ruins of great castles of the Barons of Alsace, which in the olden days resounded with the melodious notes of the hunter's horn, and the baying of hounds on the scent of the fleet footed stag.

Northward one finds the plains of the Zorn, bordered by the forest of Brumath; the picturesque valley of the Moder; the ancient sylvan haunt of the Hagenaus, where in the middle ages the great Charlemagne was wont to gather his knights for hunt and feast. One may follow the many charming streams throughout the province with great artistic return; for instance, the various tributaries of the Ill, such as La Laich and the Grand-Ballon. The former serves as a silver setting for the charming little industrial town of Guebwiller, whose smoking chimneys are curtained by splendid trees massed against sloping hillside vineyards all gold and green in the sunlight. Farther on is the old turreted town of Soultz, with ancient houses of quaint outside staircases, and dim streets blocked by lavishly sculptured stone fountains. They say that the old walls which formerly surrounded the town were pulled down and used in the construction of many of the houses, which indeed have no aspect of newness that one can now discover. This river La Laich empties into the Ill at Colmar.

The river Fecht, of swiftly running water, is used to run countless mills along its course to the interesting old town of Türckheim, with its old gateway—a comfortable halting place for the voyager. Within the mossy walls of the "Deux Clefs" (The Two Keys) in the sleepy square of a half forgotten town is a community of about two thousand quaintly costumed people, who are well nigh all engaged in the neighboring vineyards. One could live here in great comfort and enjoyment at a cost of three or four marks a day. Near by, on the other side of the valley, are the ruins of the castle of Hohlandsburg, destroyed in 1635, and said to be haunted by a stone throwing ghost, who, however, failed to cast one at the present chronicler.

On the river Weiss is Kaysersburg, a town noted as one of the Imperial Appanages of the ancient Décapole of Alsatia. The sketch which I made of it one Sunday morning shows better than description the character of the old byway and the quaint peaked roofed houses against the dark green hillside. See, through the old arched gateway, the entrance to the small church with its mellow-toned and creamy whitewashed walls; the lace curtained windows of the high gabled house beyond, and the iron work finials on the house tops.

Here the peasants, clad in opera bouffe costumes, linger after church, along the walled roadway bordering the half dried streamlet, discussing the sermon, the day's happenings, or what not.

At Ribeauville flows the Strengbach, called the "Pearl of the Vosges," and at Liepvrette the babbling stream laves Sainte-Marie-aux-Mines, said to be one of the richest and fairest of the towns of Haute-Alsace, rivaling Mulhouse for industry.

Beyond the valley the Leipvrette joins the Giessen, and flows into the Landgraben, an ancient ditch dug, it is said, by order of Charlemagne to delimit the Nordgau and the Sundgau departments.

"The river Rhine is the natural limit of the great Alsatian plain, but it is the river Ill which dominates it." [1]

This river Ill is born, lives and vanishes in Alsace. It has its source at a small place called Trinkel near the hamlet of Ferrette, where in a dim dark wood dwell the strange sect of Anabaptists, and the hermit-like families

[1] "Provinces Perdues," Ardouin-Dumazet.

28

of the wood cutters (*Schlitteurs*). Lost lower down in
wild rocky fissures, it appears again below the village of
Ligsdorf. Turning abruptly eastward toward Bâle, it
again changes its erratic course to the northwest toward
Altkirch and Mulhouse. At Largue it receives the
waters of a small affluent coming from the Jura, passing
the villages of Seppois-le-Bas, Moos and Dannemarie—
consecrated names in the province through their great
part in the bloody war of deliverance. At Mulhouse the
river assumes worthily her name and justifies her fame.
All the streams descending from the Vosges flow to her,
and on their way do their part in furnishing power to
the countless mills on their banks.

The greatest of these tributaries is of course the Doller,
born in the small lake called the Serven, lying among the
plateaus of the ancient moraines formed by the glaciers.
In its passage the Doller winds about such charming villages as Mase-vaux, Laun, Aspach, Burnhaupt and Dornach. There is too, the Thur, another very important
tributary on which are the quaint and busy towns of Wes-
serling, Saint-Amarine and Malmerspach in the high valley, and in the lower one, Ville, Biltchwiller, Thann (see
picture), and Vieux-Thann, all manufacturing places of
great activity and prosperity. Then that vast plain of
twenty thousand acres, the Champs-des-Boeufs (Ochsen-
feldt), which gives name to a kind of pudding much
esteemed by the people and sold at a great yearly cattle

fair, which draws great crowds of peasants and visitors from far and near.

The river Ill flowing through Strassburg empties into the Rhine near the charming village of the Wantzenau called by Edmund About the "pays des bonnes poules." He continues: "I have spoken at length of the Ill, because it is more than any other the great vital artery of Alsace. The three most populous towns, Mulhouse, Colmar and Strassburg, were born upon its banks. All the noble valleys of the Vosges open upon the plain through which it runs; all the other rivers, all the mountain torrents, the brooks unite with it, and it is thus with reason that the country lying between the Vosges and the Rhine is named Alsace—El-sass—the country of the Ill. Uniting all the streams, it penetrates to the noble city of Strassburg, where beats the heart of Alsace."

Northward of Schlestadt between Hochfelden and Strassburg one enters the gently undulating country called the Kocherberg, the rural and agricultural section where are best preserved the quaint usages and customs of ancient Alsace; where painters such as Kauffman, Henri Loux, Dove, Theophile Schuler, to mention only a few of the long list of famous names, found their genre subjects. . . . One could continue this description for pages without more than touching upon the attractions of the little community.

Of legend there are unwritten volumes to be listened

to if one is interested, and considering the important place that the culture of the grape has in the life of the province, it is not strange that most of them are connected in some way with the product. There is too great rivalry between the different vineyards. One of the local songs is as follows:

"A Thann dans la 'Rangen'
A Guebwiller dans la 'Wann'
A Türckheim dans la 'Brand'
Croissant les meilleurs du pays,
Mais a Riquewihr le 'Sporen'
Leur dame a tous le pion."

At Hunawihr there is a most curious specimen of fortified church, near which gushes forth a fountain dedicated to and named for Saint Huna, who was, according to the legend, a chatelaine of the place. Follows the legend: Once upon a time the blight fell upon the vineyards here, and there were no grapes to be gathered. The people in consequence were near starvation, and in their extremity flocked to the Saint, beseeching succor at her hands. They came in procession through the crooked streets of the town crying aloud their woes. It may be imagined that Saint Huna could not remain deaf to such piteous supplications on the part of her people, and lo! even as the first peasant set foot upon the threshold of the church, the miracle happened. From the four spouts of the old fountain before the door gushed forth good red wine, in such profusion that every receptacle, cask, tub, pail and pitcher in the town was filled to the brim and "there never was so much wine before or since in the community." So fell the legend from the lips of an old dame, who sat knitting in the sun on the steps of the sacred fountain of Hunawihr.

The natural chasm of the Vosges is heightened by countless ruins of the great feudal castles and monasteries with which it abounds. Perhaps no other region in Europe contains so many as are to be found on these rugged high hills, which form something of a natural defense against the German enemy. These ruined "Châteaux-fortes" reveal to the educated eye of the antiquary Celtic, Gallic, or Romanic types of construction, in all their varieties. One may study the ruins of the Châteaux of Spesburg; of Girbaden; Birkenfels; d'Andlau; Driestein and Landsberg; all near Sainte-Odile, crowned with its great convent.

"In the Belfort region alone there are at least a hundred noble ruins to be found, where great courts are carpeted now with green moss, and the walls are curtained with ivy. At Engelburg the great Donjon is still to be seen, where through the hole in the large mass of stone set upright on its side, which is called by the superstitious peasantry 'The Eye of the Sorcerer,' a magnificent view of the dim valley is to be had. Near Guebwiller are the remains of the renowned Abbey of Murbach of the Roman period, with two great towers surmounting a transept. Also the 'Trois-châteaux' of Eguisheim, where Leon IX, son of Hugues IV, Count of Eguisheim and Ida of Dagsbourg, descendants of Charlemagne in the maternal line, and Ethicon, Duke of Alsace, father of Sainte Odile, and ancestor of five dynasties of Europe—Hapsburg, Suabia, Bourbon, Lorraine and Baden, was born." [1]

The list of châteaux is far too long to include here, but one must name Sainte-Odile, with its ancient "mur païen," called the heart of mystic Alsace, from whose summit is revealed the smiling valleys of Sainte-Marie and Ville, of Ortenberg and the Ramstein, and the deep dark forests of Lutzelbourg, Kapfel, Klingenthal, Hagelschloss, Ratsamhausen, Hagenfels, Birkenfels, Driestein, Andlau, Spesburg and Landsberg.

At Hoh-Bar Château in the Savern country dwelt the great Bishops of Strassburg. This castle dominates the whole valley of the Zorn. Here is the famed mount of Savern, still bordered by the row of venerable poplars so admired by Louis XIV.

But this little sketch cannot pretend to give a complete list of the famous places and ancient castles of Alsace, nor to describe their glories. Suffice it if one can simply whet the appetite, for the feast that is offered, by this account of a little known region.

[1] " 'L'Alsace." Leon Boll (Directeur du *Journal d'Alsace-Lorraine*), Paris.

ALSACE-LORRAINE

In a chapter written by M. Daniel Blumenthal, former Mayor of Colmar, for the book "L'Alsace-Lorraine," he says: "The Germans and the Alsatians can never meet upon common ground because the Teutonic mind is absolutely irreconcilable with the delicate sensibility of that of the Alsatian. The Teuton has absolutely no sense of humor and lacks tact. When the Germans took possession of the provinces after the war, the various officials sought to rule by force, and with entire disregard of the established usages and traditions of the country. This lack of grace and tact wounded the spirits of the Alsatians, and killed at once and forever whatever feeling of tolerance they may have had for the invaders. The Teuton is ever and above all a man of violence, and the new official heads of the various municipal departments began at once a regime of persecution and punishment against the unfortunate people for the most petty and futile causes. The singing of the tune or words of the 'Marseillaise,' or having in one's possession the colors of France, was sufficient to cause the arrest and punishment of the offender."

He continues, "I recall the case of the two young fellows, who being a trifle the worse for drink during a 'patronale fête,' cried 'Vive la France' in the hearing of a gend'arme, who thereupon arrested and haled them before the German magistrate, who promptly sentenced them to eighteen months' imprisonment. The German administrators of 'Justice' are repeatedly shown by well-known cases to be absolutely incapable of impartiality where an Alsatian is concerned."

Concerning the humor of the Alsatians he says: "The people never fail to seize the opportunity to make fun of the invaders. For instance, there is the legend of the mouse, which as an 'Ex voto,' may be seen hung up beside the altars of the small country churches and chapels. One day, during a 'pilgrimage,' as these fête days are called, a German officer, drawn thither by curiosity, encountered an old peasant woman near an altar, where, among the other objects and offerings, was a silver mouse. 'And what, my good woman, is that for?' he asked. The peasant explained that the country was being ravaged by rats, and in supplication to the Saint, the silver mouse was an offering and a prayer for succor and release from the pest. 'But come now,' contemptuously asked the burly officer, 'do you believe, seriously, in such incredible idiocy?' 'My good Monsieur,' responded she with a shy smile, 'if we were absolutely sure that our prayers would be granted we would long ago *have hung up* a solid gold Prussian!'"

The German Yoke

The German Yoke

ALSACE-LORRAINE territorially is only about five thousand six hundred miles in extent, say a little larger than the State of Connecticut, and with a population of about one and a half million, who really, it is urged, are, and have been since their enforced annexation and oppression, more French than the Parisians. General Foy said enthusiastically of the Alsatians, "If ever the love of all that is great and generous grows faint in the hearts of the people of France, it will be necessary only for them to pass the Vosges Mountains into Alsace to recover their patriotism and their energy."

To one statesman who complained to him that the Alsatians spoke a German patois, Napoleon replied with vehemence: "What matters that?—Though they speak German, they *saber* in French!"

Admitting that to-day only a scant third of the people habitually use the French tongue, even the most ignorant of the peasantry are conversant with French, while among the more educated and cultivated it is universal, even though after the annexation the offices of public functionaries, such as school teachers, mayors and rail-

39

road officials were appointed by Berlin, which controlled most of the institutions and dominated the press.

The authorities since then have made every endeavor to suppress and discourage the use of the French language in the province. Thus according to a decree publicly announced no school either public or private may use or teach it. Meetings either in public or private were promptly debarred from using the language; even the French theatres were closed to French plays. The ceremonies of the closing of French schools were marked by the most pathetic scenes recorded in the literature of Alsace-Lorraine. The French signs over the shops, even in the smallest towns as well as the larger ones throughout the unhappy land, were forbidden and ordered changed to German by decree publicly posted.

In Strassburg, according to record, a barber was arrested and heavily fined as an example, for refusing to take down his sign, which bore the word "Coiffeur"; but strangely enough he was permitted to use the word "Friseur" instead. A hotel keeper was commanded to paint out the word "Restaurant," and use instead the German word "Restauration." The name of Alsace-Lorraine was replaced by Elsass-Lothringen. To use the French phrase "à bientôt" was pronounced treasonable, being deemed by the authorities the expression of a hope that France should again rule Alsace-Lorraine. In fact, all salutations in French rendered the users liable to arrest and fine. Thus the usurpers relied upon the enforced and extended use of the German language in the province to prove irresistibly the essential Teutonism of the people. The book shops were forbidden to have in their possession any of the works of standard French authors; especially the books of Daudet, Erckmann-Chatrian and Edmond About were interdicted. But it may be said that these as well as many others might always be had by those purchasers vouched for by trusted persons.

Soon after the annexation the officials used every sort of trick and intrigue to detect and convict of treason such Alsatians as they wished to rid themselves of. The "Ligue des Patriotes" was formed secretly at Strassburg by loyal Frenchmen who pledged themselves to labor for the salvation of Alsace-Lorraine. The organization had no sooner begun its work than it was betrayed by a housemaid, a German spy, and the members were arrested by the police, who searched the domiciles, found and seized the records and pamphlets, and the leaders were tried by the court, convicted and sentenced to various terms of imprisonment, some receiving as much as ten years in prison for their patriotism. In protestation the inhabitants resolved to refuse to recognise or maintain any sort of social relations with the German officials.

The entertainments conducted by the Germans were scrupulously avoided by the loyal people. The

German theatres were often forced to play to empty benches, although they were kept open and running by subsidy from the Government, which used every artifice to force their plans of subjugation upon the people. Thus they sometimes selected a known patriot for some small office or honor, but should he accept he was certainly expelled from the league, and ostracised socially.

Should an Alsatian girl so far forget her vows as to espouse a German, henceforth she was disowned by her own people, and considered as one dead. Thus society dealt with the invader in the two inseparable provinces of Alsace-Lorraine.

Then fell the heavy hand of the great German military system upon the people. The larger towns became large military depots, housing thousands of soldiers in the hated uniforms. The streets were filled with marching men, and night and day heavy rumbling army wagons occupied the streets. Officers swaggered along the sidewalks arm in arm, pushing the inhabitants rudely into the gutters; they filled the cafés; they guzzled beer, were noisy, and insolent, seeking quarrels with civilians, who had no redress if attacked or insulted. No young woman was safe from their unwelcome attentions, and some of the recorded acts of these officers are well nigh unbelievable; but the details of these offenses can have no place in these pages.

THE GERMAN YOKE

Their treatment of civilians was part of the plan of subjugation. Unless young men are surreptitiously sent away into France by their parents, they can get no other education than that imposed upon them in the military training schools maintained by the German system. Thus if they succeed in evading the established rule and leave without registering at headquarters they are outlawed, and treated as deserters from military service, nor can they ever return without suffering heavy penalty and consequent imprisonment. Even in the elementary schools the young boys are formed into military companies under appointed petty officers, and forced to adopt the "goose step." The sight is ridiculous in the extreme, but woe be to him who ventures to laugh when the hapless children thus pass marching under the watchful eye of the drill-sergeant; this is an offense against the Emperor and is punishable by fine.

In the small Alsatian town of Zabern a poor crippled cobbler watched one day from his shop door a number of officers who were pompously parading the street. One of these was a very young red-faced, yellow-haired fellow, hardly more than a boy, but gorgeously clad in the uniform of a lieutenant, with dangling sword. The sight of this youth moved the poor cripple to hysterical laughter, in which some of the bystanders joined. The lieutenant turned upon him furiously and ran the crippled cobbler through the body with his sword. The cobbler died then and there.

The military authorities gravely held court martial and exonerated the lieutenant, praising him for having protected the honor of the uniform and the army. The cobbler, dead, was convicted of "lèse majesté."

The further details of the "Zabern Incident" are as follows:

In December, 1913, the Alsatians, nowhere patient of German government, had shown what was regarded by the authorities as lack of respect for the garrison troops. A young Prussian lieutenant, Von Forstner, referred to above, thereupon offered a reward of ten marks to any soldier who, if "insulted" by a native of the town, struck the offender and brought him into barracks.

In the harangue he used an insulting term to denote Alsatians; and it is worth observing, in view of what followed, that the definition of what constituted an insult was left entirely to the troops.

The nature and language of Lieutenant Von Forstner's address becoming known, there was an unfriendly demonstration by the townspeople of Zabern outside the officer's mess, which was dispersed by soldiers with loaded rifles. The lieutenant then "went out shopping," escorted by four soldiers with fixed bayonets. In the evening the popular excitement increased; whereupon the colonel of the regiment proclaimed martial law and placed machine guns in the streets. The scene which followed is thus described in the calm pages of the *Annual Register:*[1]

"A fireman who left his supper when he heard the drums of the regiment was arrested at his door; the Judge and counsel of the Civil Court, which had just risen, were also arrested as they were leaving the Court. The Judge was allowed to go home, but all the others (twenty-seven in number) spent the night in the cellars of the barracks, and were only liberated the next day, when they were brought before the Judge for trial. . . . A further aggravation of the scandal was the arrest of a man and his wife at Metz, because the wife laughed at a passing patrol." Judicial proceedings followed, in which it was proved that "When warned that his unprovoked incitement of the population was likely to lead to bloodshed," Colonel Von Reuter, who commanded Von Forstner's regiment, had said that "Bloodshed would be a good thing," and that civilians had been arrested for "Intending to laugh." The colonel was finally acquitted on the ground that "he did not know that he acted illegally." He himself based his action on a Prussian Cabinet order of the year 1820.

It must not be supposed that this example of military

[1] *The Annual Register*, 1913, p. 319.

zeal was universally approved in Germany. It aroused a storm of controversy, and the Reichstag actually passed a resolution by 293 votes to 54 declaring that it was dissatisfied with the Chancellor's rather half-hearted defense of the conduct of the garrison. But the protest of the Reichstag and the more independent sections of the public was entirely ineffectual. The Crown Prince had telegraphed to Colonel Von Reuter during his trial, exhorting him ("Immer feste darau") to "stick to it"; and General Von Falkenhayn, the Prussian Minister of War, had declared in the Reichstag that "What they had to deal with was not the degree of a lieutenant's offense, but *a determined attempt by press agitation and abuse to exercise an unlawful influence upon the decision of the authorities.*" Dr. Jagow, the Police President at Berlin, afterwards supported these views of the matter, and telegraphed to Colonel Von Reuter during his trial, "Exercises are acts of sovereignty, and if obstacles are placed in the way of their performance, the obstacles must be removed in the execution of this act of sovereignty." Dr. Jagow may be supposed, in virtue of the office he held, not to have expressed public opinion on matters of state without some idea whether those opinions were agreeable to the Government. When the pother had died down, his theory that "Military exercises"—such as running lame cobblers through the body, and shopping with fixed bayonets—"are acts of sovereignty" apparently held the field, so far as official Germany was concerned.

The very mild sentence of forty-three days' detention passed on Lieutenant Von Forstner was quashed by a higher military court, and (as we have seen) Colonel Von Reuter was decorated with a Prussian Order at the beginning of the new year. It would hardly have been possible to demonstrate more clearly that in the eyes of the German government there is one law for the army and another for civilians, and that civil must yield to military rights whenever they conflict. "One is often pained and overcome with longing" (writes a modern German professor), "as one thinks of the German of a hundred years ago. He was poor, he was impotent, he was despised, ridiculed and defrauded. He was the uncomplaining slave of others; his fields were their battleground, and the goods which he had inherited from his fathers were trodden under foot and dispersed. He never troubled when the riches of the outside world were divided without regard for him. He sat in his little bare room under the roof in simple coat and clumsy shoes; but his heart was full of sweet dreams, and uplifted by the chords of Beethoven to a rapture which threatened to rend his breast. He wept with Werther and Jean Paul in joyous pain, he smiled with the childish innocence of his naïve poets, the happiness of his longing consumed him, and as he listened to Schubert's song his

47

soul became one with the soul of the universe. Let us think no more of it—it is useless!" [1]

Germany claims that Alsace-Lorraine was German territory that was justly restored to her; that "in taking back the provinces she accomplished an act of supreme national and historic justice"; such is the utterance of the official publication of the Emperor, the *Nord-Deutsche Algemeine Zeitung.*

Is this so? In the first place, the people of Alsace-Lorraine are not all as thoroughly German as is claimed by the *Zeitung*, but those of the province who are have certainly purer German blood flowing in their veins than the pseudo-Germans—those from beyond the Elbe and the Rhine—who are certainly of a very mixed race, indeed, authorities say, somewhat more than sixty per cent. Slav. German lust for Alsace-Lorraine was very evident even in the days of Julius Cæsar. In his "Commentaries" one may read of the Teutonic covetousness for the lands of the Sequanians, who occupied what is now Alsace-Lorraine.

"Ariovistus, the king of the Germans, had settled in their territory, and had seized upon one third of it, the best land in the whole of Gaul; and now he demanded that the natives should vacate another third, because a few months previously twenty four thousand Harndes

[1] "Der Kaiser und die Zukunft des deutschen Volks." By G. Fuchs, pp. 70–71.

had joined him, and he had to find homestead lands for them. Within a few years the entire population of Gaul would be expatriated, and the Germans would all cross the Rhine; for there was no comparison between the land of the Germans and that of the Sequanians, or between the standard of living among the former and that of the latter."

Other and much more odious characteristics than those of covetousness of their neighbors' lands seem to unite the Germans of that remote day with those of to-day.

"Ariovistus had wrapped himself in so much haughtiness," says Cæsar, "that he had become unbearable. These wild barbarians had become enamored of the lands and refinements and abundance of the Gauls, and more were brought over until about one hundred and twenty thousand of them were in Gaul." Cæsar attacked, put them to flight, and drove them back beyond the Rhine.

The people were thus Gallo-Romans, and not Teuton. The hegemony which the German kings obtained over a great part of Europe was obtained by them as Roman emperors and not as monarchs of Germany. These two titles should not be confused. Lorraine formed part of the Holy Roman Empire, but not of Germany. But leaving out altogether the period of the Middle Ages, and coming down to more modern times, we find that when Prussia seized Alsace-Lorraine in 1871 these two provinces had been French possessions since 1648; that is to say, for a period of 233 years. But apart from any consideration of priority of the length of time of possession, there is a very important question involved. The Rhine now and always has marked the natural division between Germany and France, and not until the invader has been driven back across this permanent division will this cause be abandoned. Then there is the even stronger consideration—the moral right which the French have to Alsace-Lorraine. By their civilization, which they inherit from their beloved France—by their ardent affection—by their never-dying hope to belong once more to France, these patriotic people proclaim to the world that they are not Germans, and that the yoke imposed upon them is insufferable.

The patriot Jonas Lippman relates how in afflicted Alsace the Teuton conquerors have repeatedly stopped the performance of French musical comedies and even expelled French actors from the province, threatening them with imprisonment should they dare to return without written permission.

"It has been," he says, "my bad fortune to see at Strassburg a performance of 'La Fille du Regiment' stopped by the police. The German excuse was that when the 'Daughter of the Regiment' displays the French flag this constitutes a seditious manifestation! At another time an advertised performance of 'Faust' was prohibited because of the well known chorus 'Gloire

Immortelle de nos aieux,' 'which,' so read the report of the police authorities, 'was an attempt to recall to an Alsatian audience the glory of their French ancestors.'"

Another instance of persecution was the expulsion from Alsace of the great French comedian the elder Coquelin, who came to play in Molière's "Precieuses Ridicules." No official reason was given for that expulsion. He was given two hours to leave Strassburg. Coquelin was an intimate friend of the great Gambetta, and that was enough!

"On the thirtieth day of September, 1870," continues M. Lippman, "we inhabitants of Strassburg heard for the last time the French 'Clairon,' and for the first time the Prussian trumpet. Napoleon III had declared war on Prussia on the 15th of July; four weeks after that the enemy surrounded Strassburg and closed it to the world. On the 13th of August the first shell was fired on the city, at 1 o'clock, and from that time on till the 28th of September a continuous bombardment was kept up. The word continuous is here used in its most exact meaning. Not once did the Prussian batteries relent in their deadly work. The inhabitants took refuge in their cellars, the dampness of which increased the already high mortality. We lived there in disagreeable promiscuity, all the tenants of the house forming a congregation, as it were, of suffering humanity. Men, women, and children, old and young, patricians and plebeians, Catholics and Jews,

Protestants and infidels, a vivid illustration showing that misery loves company. And what a weird company! A University professor tête-à-tête with a plumber; a silk merchant having as vis-a-vis a mail carrier; a piano manufacturer fraternizing with an undertaker—and so on. The women fared no better. Separated from the men by a rude sort of curtain, if I may so call it, they had troubles of their own in taking care of the children. There were enough of them to form a kindergarten. In ordinary times the noise of so many youngsters would have been unbearable, but at this time no one paid any attention to it. The fearful crashing and exploding of shells over our roofs, followed by a rain of debris which made the streets impossible, rendered us at times speechless, but did not in the least disturb the children. Occasionally we would hear the cries above, 'Au feu! Au feu!' when a nearby building caught fire. In normal times when one heard that cry he would summon the nearest post of firemen, who with their old fashioned equipment—a few yards of hose and a hand pump—would trot leisurely to the burning building followed by a crowd yelling, 'Au feu! Au feu!' But during such a bombardment the cry found no echo—no one ventured to cross the street, as it meant sure death. Besides, the men who composed the Fire Department were on duty on the ramparts, and their places had been taken by amateur volunteers who were unwilling to risk their lives without benefit to their fellow citizens, for the Teutons invariably concentrated the fire of their batteries upon that particular spot, so as to prevent any help.

"The office of public announcer or town crier during these days was not a sinecure. In the towns of Alsace-Lorraine the crier (*crieur publique*) appears at certain hours of the day to read at each street corner announcements which the authorities wish to impart officially to the citizens. The crier beats loudly upon a drum for a few moments to collect a crowd, to whom he then reads his document in a loud sing-song voice. During the bombardment of 1870 there was considerable danger in the performance of that duty. For us residents of the cellars the beating of the official drum (he says) created a diversion. Our curiosity was quickly aroused. We crawled out of our caverns, walked up to the front door, but did not dare to venture further. The announcement consisted usually of a communication from the Mayor, or from the Military Governor of Strassburg, informing the inhabitants 'that they would soon be relieved, that a French army was battering its way to succor them, and recommending them to keep up courage.' Some of us on hearing the communication felt encouraged, others shook their heads; but no one dared to hint at surrender. We returned to our damp holes, optimists and pessimists, awaiting events.

"On the 8th day of September—Thursday—the pub-

lic crier pounded more heavily than usual upon his drum.
We took up our vantage points and were startled when,
in a deep trembling voice, the old man (did I tell you
that he was an old man?) read as follows:

" 'Dear fellow citizens: The French Army, after a
brilliant battle lasting two days, outnumbered five to
one, has suffered defeat at Sedan. Napoleon III has
surrendered his sword to the King of Prussia before his
troops. The Emperor is a prisoner of war. A Republic
has been proclaimed at Paris. The Empress has fled to
England. A Provisional Government has been formed
to prosecute the war. People of Strassburg, the Imperial régime has ceased, but France remains. Vive la
France!' "

" 'Yes, Vive la France!' shouted the University Professor—'and also Vive la République!' 'So then,'
commented the cave dwellers, 'that is what Napoleon
III has done for us! Unprepared, unequipped, he declared war upon Prussia, and to-day we are at the mercy
of a cruel enemy! The Imperial Régime left no regrets
in Republican Alsace. . . .' Paris and Strassburg
were compelled to surrender by starvation.

"In 1870 we lacked milk for our babies. Leading citizens signed a petition begging General Von Werder, the
Commander of the invading Prussian forces, to 'please
let us have milk for our wounded, for our aged, for our
babies.' He answered, 'Ergibt euch wenn Ihr milch

wollt.' (Surrender if you want milk.) In those days substitutes for milk were not known, so that hundreds of our babies died of starvation. No Alsatian has forgotten it.

"The situation became more acute," (continues M. Lippman); "besides the lack of food, the bombardment became unbearable. Prussian batteries did not confine their shots to the ramparts or the fortifications. Nothing was sacred to them. Entire streets of Strassburg—residential sections—were burned; public buildings, churches, monuments became the prey of Prussian vandalism. The Theatre, the Museum, the Prefecture, the Protestant Church called the Temple Neuf with its great Library containing treasures of Latin MSS., the roof of the world famous Cathedral—all these monuments became smoking, smouldering ruins under Prussian shells. We were wondering what the end would be when, on September 28th, the cannon stopped. It was five o'clock in the afternoon. The silence, strange as it may seem, became uncomfortable. We ventured out on the street, walked over the debris, tobogganing would better express it, and met a little group of people craning their necks up at the Cathedral tower. We saw that the Tricolor had been hauled down. In its place a white cloth was hanging. I was too young at the time to realize what it all meant. My father, who had me by the hand, was shaking like a leaf. I asked him the cause of the excitement and he replied: 'You see "ce chiffon blanc" (that white rag)? It is the flag of dishonor—of shame —of humiliation! It means that to-morrow the Prussians will be our masters.' And to-morrow came! Whoever has not seen a city surrendered to the enemy —and what an enemy!—cannot grasp what it means. No Zola, no De Maupassant—no Daudet can adequately describe the thousand and one emotions that electrify one as one sees his beloved ones lined up in a public square prepared to go into captivity, while at the same time he hears in the distance the strains of military bands preceding the victorious troops entering the beloved town. The vandals robbed us of our Strassburg by sheer brutal force. No Alsatian has forgiven, or ever will forgive, that Prussian Crime!"

. . . Written all over the plains, hills, and valleys of Alsace-Lorraine in ancient ruins, prehistoric monuments and stone piles, is the epic of the land already old when Cæsar came. The remains of Druid temples still stand even to-day beside the crumbling stones marking the site of walls built by the Romans. On Mount Ste. Odile is the beginning of a colossal bulk of uncemented blocks of great stones stretching across leagues of hill and valley. The ancient annals are scanty and often incoherent, but enough can be gathered to prove that the Germans gradually occupied the territory by what is called "peaceful

penetration," which later became domination and Teu-
tonified "Alsace" into "Ellsass." Then followed the
towns of Metz, Altkirch, and Strassburg, which the Germans point to as proof that the Teuton was the dominant
force in both Alsace and Lorraine. But the governing
power was settled very definitely at, and by, the treaty
of Verdun, A. D. 843 and attested manually by the Sons
of Charlemagne. Of the three sons signatory to this
document, Lothaire received and became proprietor of
Alsace, Lorraine, Burgundy, Provence, and some territory in Italy. This became the Kingdom of Lothaire
(Lotharii regnum) Lorraine in French, Lothringen in
German.

Upon the death of Lothaire, Charles the Bold took
Alsace, and Lorraine was seized by Louis the German,
as set forth in the curious documents ratifying these
seizures and written in both French and German. Under an agreement twenty-seven years later by the
brothers, Alsace was ceded by Charles the Bold to Louis
the German, and thus the Vosges became the boundary
between Germany and France.

In the centuries that passed, Alsace, so fair and fertile,
and Lorraine, so rich in its mines, grew rapidly in renown, attracting workmen from other less favored localities, so that soon towns and villages sprang up as if
by magic. These led to the foundation of the great feu-

dal systems, and jealously guarded communities over-lorded by Bishops, Prefects, and both Dukes and Arch-dukes.

These built their castles on the shaggy crests of the Vosges, and the ruins are still pointed out to the tourist.

It is said that the name Hapsburg was derived from one of these strongholds. The story is that the brother of the Bishop of Strassburg, out hunting one day with his hawk or falcon, followed it to a part of the country which seemed to him so beautiful that he built a castle there and named it for his falcon—"habicht"—Habichts-burg. This, in time, became Hapsburg. This house ruled Alsace until 1679, when all its rights and titles in the province were transferred to Louis XIV of France.

Wars, both great and small, swept over the provinces, and often the peasants, starving and desperate, rose against their lords. All over this fair land the ruins of the great medieval castles are surrounded by the un-marked graves of millions of unfortunate peasants whose ill-paid labor erected these huge piles of masonry over which tourists now marvel.

Even in the middle ages Alsace-Lorraine suffered from and was torn by complications which arose among the rulers. Besides the numberless seigneuries, certain of the towns claimed the right of self administration, and formed themselves into independent states, under the protection of an official called "Landvogt," a sort of Grand Bailiff appointed by the King of Germany.

Ten of these towns in the year 1353 grouped themselves into a league or confederation for mutual defense, and styled themselves the Décapole (from two Greek words signifying ten towns). Running from north to south these were: Landau, Wissembourg, Haguenau, Rosheim, Obernai, Schlestadt, Kaysersberg, Colmar, Türckheim, and Munster.

The town of Landau, reunited to France in 1648 in the "Palatinat," was ceded to Bavaria after the "cent jours," by the second treaty of Paris, in 1815.

Wissembourg, situated on the river Lauter, freed herself, after a long and weary struggle, from the domination of the Abbey, and gladly joined the league.

Haguenau, near the great forest, at the end of the fifteenth century was one of the most important of the cities of the Province of Alsace-Lorraine. It had a great château on an island in the river Moder, in which dwelt Frederic Barberousse with his knights, and it was famous for its great and beautiful Church of Saint Georges, as well as for its celebrated master printers, who produced works which are still unrivaled.

Rosheim, which possessed one of the most remarkable Roman churches throughout the country, constructed in the eleventh century, was renowned for the character and integrity of its inhabitants.

Obernai (Oberehnheim) boasted of the beauty of its

mansions situated on the river Ehn, most of which dated from the fifteenth century.

Schlestadt was famed for its colleges and its learned men. It boasted of more than eleven hundred students in the sixteenth century, under such masters as Dringen-berg, Beatus Rhenanus, and Jacob Wimpferling. The great library of Schlestadt contained more precious MSS. than any other, so it is said.

Kaysersberg, famed for its great château, where Gei-ler, the celebrated preacher at the Cathedral of Strass-burg, passed the days of his childhood.

Colmar, the painters' town, renowned for the number of celebrated artists born within its walls.

Türckheim, on the borders of the beautiful river Fecht, and renowned the land over for its noble wine, the town nestling behind great stone walls topped by quaint towers.

And lastly: Munster, at the end of the valley at the foot of the Schlucht.

Each of these towns had and enjoyed its own consti-tution, and named the magistrates charged with their government, some elected for life, and others for cer-tain periods only. These magistrates were chosen from among both the nobles and the "bourgeoisie" or citizens' class. The population was formed of a number of "tribes"; those called "Zünfte," which were very numer-ous, and were divided into clans, and the "Stubé" (poêle). Each of these had its own place. The

"Stubés" were celebrated for the family fêtes, such as marriages, christenings, etc. These two tribes elected their own head men, and a sort of major domo whom they called "Obristzunftmeister," and who was consulted in all important matters relating to the wellbeing of the tribes.

These magistrates were charged with the overseeing of the fortifications, the upkeep of arms and ordnance; the care of the streets, and the order and peace of the town. They levied the town taxes and collected them, and upon occasion acted as petty judges. The "bourgeoisie" formed the committees which governed the hospitals, the orphan asylums, and the schools. Thus they prospered and flourished in the enjoyment of liberty.

In the sixteenth century certain of the towns, for instance, Munster, Landau and Wissembourg, were converted to Protestantism, but Colmar was favorable to both Catholic and Protestant, giving them equal rights. Finally, after some dissension in the first named towns, they united in the faith of the ancient church, and thus have remained.

The Alsatian towns for many years managed to keep free from entanglements, while busied with the unsettled conditions due to the Thirty Years' religious war and the occupation by Sweden. The protection of France was gladly welcomed, and the people became so whole-heartedly French that upon the dawn of the Revolution they entered into it body and soul, furnishing both states-men and soldiers. They remained, however, cold to the advances of Napoleon III, whose ambitions they dis-trusted. . . . Then came the defeats of Wissembourg and Woerth; the bombardment of Strassburg; the Prus-sian occupation; the eloquent declarations of the deputies of Alsace-Lorraine in the assembly at Bordeaux—their protestation after the vote for the preliminaries of peace —the treaty of Frankfort, signed on May 10th, 1871, when the larger part of Alsace and a portion of Lorraine were separated from the Mother Country and designated by the hated German name of "Elsass-Lothringen," which Frenchmen cannot and will not use. Belfort and Delle remained to France.

Alsace-Lorraine then, by what the French term "un bizarre statut," became by the law of June 9, 1871, the collective property of the German States Confederation, a part of the Empire (Reichsland) and under the domi-nation and government of the princes of Ruess and Schwarzburg. It was proclaimed by these princes that Alsace-Lorraine, thus violated, was simply German ter-ritory reclaimed, that in thought and sentiment the people were Germans, and that only the interests of the people were sought and considered by the German Empire. In refutation of this specious argument it is necessary to chronicle here some of the persecutions inflicted upon these helpless people, the interdiction of the French language in the schools; the fines and punishment for displaying or even having in one's possession the French colors; the odious measures regarding passports at the French frontier; the surveillance of the police, furnished with power of domiciliary visits at any and all hours of the day or night; the insolence of the Germans sent into the country as settlers; the outrage of (Zabern) Saverne by the military. Indeed, fresh evidence of the German campaign of terrorization of the Province comes to hand every day. Since the beginning of hostilities (August, 1914,) German courts martial, sitting in the annexed provinces, have inflicted sentences totaling five thousand years' imprisonment on citizens of Alsace and Lorraine, whose sole offence has been the expression of opinions favorable to France. In this all classes and all districts have suffered.

According to carefully gathered statistics, from the day Alsace-Lorraine was annexed by Germany in 1871 until the outbreak of the World War, no fewer than five hundred thousand of the inhabitants of the provinces, out of a population of 1,600,000, have migrated to France. Of these nearly fifty thousand have joined the French army, and are fighting under the Tri-color. So the wall which the Teutons erected on the frontier in 1871 is a monument to the fidelity of the Alsatians. In words of Jaures, "They (the Teutons) have erected a monument in the depths of the forest, among the great trees whose

roots are deep in French soil, and whose branches reach
to the skies. The forest is typical of our soul. The
monument shall never fall until the lost provinces of
Alsace-Lorraine are re-united to our beloved France, and
the Tri-color waves in Strassburg on the Rhine.''

The Alsatian dialect is very peculiar and most difficult
for a foreigner to learn. This song [1] will give a good
idea of its characteristics.

I

Das Elsass unser Ländel
Das isch meineidig scheen;
Mer hewa's fescht am Bändel,
Un lehn's, bigott, mit gehn
   I uhé!
Mer lehn's, bigott, mit gehn.

II

Es sott's nur einer wage
Un sott'es grifan an,
Mer halta fescht zusamme
Un schlaga mann für man
   I uhé!
Un schlaga mann für mann.

III

Im Elsass îsch güat lawa,
Das wissen alle Leüt,
Das giebt es Feld und Rewa,
Was eim das Herz erfreut
   I uhé!
Was eim das Herz erfreut.

[1] From "Chansons Populaires de l'Alsace." Jean Maisonneuve, Edit.

THE GERMAN YOKE

IV

Steigt man auf hohe Berge
Schaut ab in's tiefe Thal,
Da seeht man Gottes Werke
Un Länder îwerall
   I uhé!
Un Länder îwerall.

V

Drum liâwa mi'r under Ländel
Mir alle Elsässer Seehn,
Und halta's fescht am Bändel
Un lehn's, bigott, nît gehn,
   I uhé!
Un lehn's, bigott, nît gehn.

Ferrette, a Toy Village

Ferrette, a Toy Village

THE charming little village of Ferrette is reached from Altkirch by a toy train of two or three miniature cars drawn by an absurd squatty engine, all gaily picked out in red and green paint. In German it is spelled Pfirt, and pronounced as comically by the quaintly garbed, red faced, and shy conductor, who obligingly gave me a card emblazoned with the name of the inn, the "Stadt New York," which he recommended with an emphatic nod of his close cropped head.

Pfirt or Ferrette is a typical village of the Sundgau region, so renowned for its picturesqueness and its pottery. The toy train puffed its way along the route in so leisurely a manner that one had ample opportunity to see in detail the rich rolling country and mark its great difference to the landscape of higher Alsace.

The large and open valley, with its prairie spaces, presents a great contrast to the Valleys of the Vosges, whose slopes are so masked by heavy dark forests. Here the villages are more isolated—farther apart, and the châlets remind one of those in Switzerland. Proceeding so slowly towards the foothills, the slow little train covers the fifteen miles to Pfirt or Ferrette all too soon.

A sort of outskirt to the village, consisting of a few châlets, first appears, called by the inhabitants (so explains the conductor) the "faubourg." Here is a heavy mass of trees, in which are vast flocks of rooks. The village itself is hidden from view, but one can see above, on a steep wooded cliff, the ruin of an ancient château—the castle of Pfirt, formerly the seat and stronghold of the Counts of Pfirt, who in olden days dominated the whole Jura mountains. Nothing could be more enchanting than the view of this old ruin on the summit of the embowered cliff, shining in the golden glow of an August evening.

Ferrette proved to be a worthy setting for the old castle, and though it had few more than five hundred inhabitants, all told, they all seemed to have congregated in the small, clean square that evening. The reason for the gathering proved to be the arrival of a moving picture show, then a great novelty, and men were busily erecting a large tent in the open space. Here was a charming old church, erected upon a quaint, grassy walled and buttressed eminence approached by a flight of stone steps which wound delightfully about the old mossy walls of steep roofed and galleried houses. The church had a tower surmounted by a singular sort of pent roof, for all the world like unto the cocked hat worn by the old Sergeant de Ville, who was then on guard, superintending the erection of the moving picture tent, with a dubious and watchful eye upon the boys who excitedly studied the operation.

This sort of church roof is remarkable in this region of bulbous and pyramidal belfries, and reminds one of those commonly seen in Normandy. The village street of Ferrette, delightfully named the "Boulevarde," is along the terrace, which overlooks the valley and the quaint pent roofs of the old houses descending the hillside in steps. A polite villager took pains to point out to us the Hôtel de Ville, which he gravely informed us was "of the fifteenth-sixteenth century, but somewhat modern likewise, because it was newly furnished this very year!" He pointed out the roadway at one side by which we could mount to the château above the village, and volunteered the information that we would first pass through the seignorial donjon of the Counts of Ferrette; that Louis XIV in 1659 gave the Seigneurié to Mazarin, whose landmarks, bearing the arms of the Cardinal, are still to be found in the neighboring forests. After Mazarin, he said, the Valentinois inherited the domain, then the Grimaldis, and that at present the Prince of Monaco enjoys, among other titles, that of a Count of Ferrette. Later we discovered that this erudite villager was none other than Monsieur the Mayor himself. From the terrace of the château the view of the country round about forms one of the most unique and moving spectacles in all Alsace. The gap of the Rhine valley between the Vosges and the Black Forest lay bathed in tender, lambent, misty light, and nearer were the golden green undulating fields of the Alsatian Jura. The whole region is peopled and filled with knights and warriors, their deeds of prowess and valor; their loves and their ladies, as well as tales of giants and dwarfs, and dragons ferocious.

Monsieur the Mayor, we afterward discovered, enjoyed a local reputation as historian of the region of the Sundgau, and although a German official appointed by Berlin, was secretly a pronounced and loyal Alsatian in feeling. To him I owe a great many of the facts and details set down in this random description of both Ferrette and Altkirch.[1]

In his quaint home he had a most unique collection of china and ancient carved furniture, in which he took an almost childish delight, and this was not the least of his attractions. He was really a mine of information concerning the country and the people. Telling the story of Altkirch in floriated language, for which he showed great fondness, he said that the name of this most picturesque town clinging to the slope of the sun-bathed hill on the Swiss frontier came from the old church erected in the year 1050 by Hugues the Venerable Abbé of Cluny, after a visit which he paid to Louis the Count of Mont-

---

[1] This kindly gentleman died the year following my visit to Ferrette. (Author.)

beliard, and his Lady Sophie de Bar, the ancestors of the Counts of Ferrette, who so long dominated upper Alsace.

It seems that the good Abbé, ever a man of moods, as well as extreme holiness, desired one day to have his dinner served to him out of doors beneath the great trees, but soon it came on to rain, seeing which the Abbé got down upon his knees before the statue of the Saint and prayed him loudly and eloquently for fair weather and bright sunlight, "when behold: The sun shone forth, the clouds vanished, and all nature smiled!"

The son of Louis Thierry sojourning here between Ferrette and Altkirch was miraculously cured of "a grave malady," and in gratitude he erected a monastery in the neighborhood, and later, the Grand Abbey of Cluny, which was dedicated to Saint Christopher under the name of Saint Moraud, in remembrance of a most holy man who came here during the twelfth century and preached the Holy Gospel to the inhabitants of the Sundgau, who even to the present day venerate him as patron Saint.

The remains of the great Abbey on the hillside are now used as a "hospice," sheltering a few quaintly clad monks, who till the well-kept gardens and care for the walled orchard in the intervals of prayer.

Altkirch

Altkirch

ALTKIRCH passed from the control of the Counts of Ferrette to the house of Hapsburg of Austria, and in 1659 was presented by France to Cardinal Mazarin. Away back in the dim days of 1375 the hordes of Enguerrand de Coucy occupied the town for three months, after which they sacked and burned it. Captured by the Armagnacs in 1444, the little town again suffered by pillage and fire, and two years later the Balois encamped here with their troops. Two hundred years later, the Swedes invaded the region, leaving in their wake little but ragged walls. But both Ferrette and Altkirch survived these disasters, and even became rich and famed the country round. Under the French régime in the twelfth century, Altkirch's great annual Fair, celebrated in the month of July, enjoyed much renown. Its narrow, tortuous streets were thronged with rich merchants, and its square, surrounded by quaint gabled houses, was covered with well stocked booths containing rich stuffs from the looms of Flanders, while outside the stone walls surrounding the town great droves of sleek and blooded cattle and fine Norman horses were offered for sale, attracting buyers from far and near. Thus a great prosperity settled upon the town, and its merchants and inhabitants waxed rich and proud.

From 1800, Altkirch, down to 1857, was a "sous prefecture" of the Upper Rhine, but in the latter year this title was removed and bestowed upon Mulhouse. Altkirch was the seat of an excellent college, and here was educated the painter Jean Jacques Henner, who was born at Bernwiller, a neighboring village.

The Henner family were very poor, with many children, but they sent young Henner to Strassburg to study art. Later he went to Paris, where he became famous. He never forgot his birthplace, however, and regularly visited his parents, whom he was able to care for in their old age. In his paintings he depicted often the Alsatian type of face with the picturesque headdress. After he died, in 1905, his friends and admirers erected a monument to him in Bernwiller. "And now," continued our historian, "Altkirch is famed for its charming pottery, not perhaps as magnificent as that of Sèvres, but nevertheless of good quality and design, and I hope that M'sieur and Madame will agree with me as to its quality." He looked so beseeching and anxious for the compliment, that Lady Anne hastened to agree with him for politeness' sake. I remember a quaint figure of speech of Miss Wharton's describing a French town: "It has been the fate of many venerable towns to sacrifice their bloom of 'Vetuste' to the restoring craze, which gives them the pathetic appearance of cosseted old ladies and antediluvian beaux, parading their makeups." But no one need pity Altkirch, it is as redolent of untouched antiquity as one could wish, and it was our good luck to be here on a market day, when the streets were full of bright-eyed peasant girls, and lively merchants; and drivers in quaint smocks and broad-brimmed hats, as well as some in the quaint old tasseled caps of velvet worn rakishly far back on the head by the men from the more remote villages. Climbing some of the steep streets, we wondered what was occurring behind the high walls of those gabled, steep-roofed houses, to which the tourist so rarely has access.

Little life was visible at the curtained windows, save occasionally the wrinkled face of an old velvet-capped woman. The gray old church seemed withdrawn immeasurably into the dim past, sunk in the forgotten memories of ancient Gaul, and even the chanting circle of children, dancing a kind of "ring around the rosy" before the steps, were as subdued and well mannered as befitted the scene.

In the old church the effect of this antiquity was enhanced by what one might call beneficent neglect. Here were all the scars and hues of age, untouched by the restorer. The old choir, the organ loft and rood screen, all

79

of a lacy yet heavy woodcarving, have preserved well their detail, acquiring with the centuries that precious lustre of surface that one associates with the patina of old bronze. It was unfinished, of course; all great Gothic temples are unfinished—always will be; *"Dieu Merci!"* —with something left to the imagination—and this old church quite satisfied one's æsthetic sense in that respect.

The people of Altkirch are very French in manner. All those whom we encountered, from the people at the "Blume," noted for its comforts, to the white-aproned baker who was arranging a fragrant pile of cakes in his open window, were smiling and good-humored, and the little old man in the stiff blue blouse at the inn, who was draining the lettuce in a wire cage, which he swung about his head, each pursued his activities with cheerful acceptance of the conditions attached to their several occupations. Each was apparently conscious of his established walk of life and gloried in it.

We could not but admire this characteristic, this really admirable fitting of each member of the community into the fabric of everyday existence. It must be the outcome of their admirable sense of form, lubricated by the good manners possessed by the French, which doubtless has led them by a short cut to their goal.

It was difficult for one to leave the attractions of Altkirch and the picturesque fertile valley adorned by many old embowered châteaux and farmsteads, built when reminiscences only lingered from those good old times when private feuds armed every man against his neighbor, and made every mansion a stronghold. These assumed an intermediate character between fortress and peaceful habitation. Their glazed windows were in strange proximity to flanking towers and iron-plated and nail-studded doors. But they were most pleasing features in the landscape, and with their high steep roofs garnished with two or three rows of curious little dormer windows, and iron pinnacles of every imaginable design, often most artistic, their character added immensely to the picture, as when, for instance, placed upon a projecting bluff almost surrounded by a swiftly running stream.

In exploring the valley one day, we found the road thronged with pilgrims on their way to or from a shrine, we did not ascertain which. The greater number were on foot, in scattered parties, but later on we met with the procession marching in two files. The children came first, generally clad in white and carrying banners and emblems. Those who followed seemed to march in the order of their age. Between the files were the priests, in full regalia. A crucifix was borne in advance of the whole train, and an ornate painted and embroidered banner at the head of each file. They were either singing hymns or reciting prayers. We were told that these processions at night were most beautiful and impressive, and that the most attractive sight of all the poetic scenes which the festival presented was when the pilgrims, lighted by the glare of torches, embarked in large barges and floated down the river with their banners and sacred symbols all displayed, making the night resound with the sweet voices of the women and children and the deep responses of the chanting priests and choristers.

It is not to be supposed that such ceremonies and spectacles as this should fail to arouse an anxious interest and bitter antipathy among the German Protestants of Alsace, and it is perhaps enough to say here that every obstacle and discouragement is put in the way of such innocent celebrations by the civic authorities, under secret orders from Berlin. But to the casual observer this is, of course, hidden, and on the surface the village life goes on placidly; suffice it for him that this is a romantic region of mountains and fair valleys, with tossing water courses and thick forests abounding in rare plants; of grand rivers flowing through rocky chasms or lovely meadow lands, and gemmed by such marvelous old towns and villages as transport those who visit and tarry in them into the Middle Ages; where the sunny uplands are dotted by such a lavish wealth of ruined castles and half forgotten abbeys and the remains of charming châteaux, as to be well nigh impossible to chronicle or describe. Rarely did we meet with an English traveller after crossing the French frontier, save for two elderly English ladies who were discovered economising in a delightfully remote inn on the flowery banks of the Ill. Both were quite "midvictorian," wearing lace head-dresses at dinner, and as coldly dignified in deportment as one can well imagine. And it is quite true that one happened upon the rosy-cheeked maid in the hallway bearing a tray up to their apartment at nine o'clock in the evening, upon which was a steaming pitcher of milk and a fat squat bottle of "Hollands."

"Yes, indeed," said the maid most earnestly, "these great ladies, after the fashion of the English, must have each night before retiring the gin and hot milk. It is the manner of the nobility in their country. They are great ladies, you understand? It is for them that we have the 'ros' biff,' and also, on occasion, the 'plum pud-dang.' The ladies are here for the season, and we love them, too." Delightful hospitality!

It seemed strange that more travellers did not resort to these charming inns. Nowhere else perhaps could one live so cheaply and withal so free from care, and be so hospitably received and entertained.

Was it not Smollett who complained so bitterly be-cause at a French inn a "diner apart" cost him three francs, while the charge for the "table d'hôte" was only forty sous? It was because the landlords discouraged such exclusiveness. The table d'hôte is an estab-lished institution and a most excellent and entertaining one too. True, the ubiquitous commercial traveller is not always the most pleasant of companions at table, but your experienced globe trotter learns to take what comes and all uncomplainingly.

These provincial inns are, as a rule, excellently well kept. The beds are invariably immaculately clean, with splendid linen, woven often in the neighborhood. The food is excellent and well cooked, and the chamber into which the traveller is welcomed has almost invariably the heavy furniture which was once thought indispensable to every well furnished salon. In the center of the room will be the heavy marble-topped table (guéridon), with its square of embroidery upon which is a vase for flowers. Upon the mantel will be a clock of the empire under a glass dome, showing some hero or other in bronze, upon either side of which is a gilt vase of artificial flowers, likewise under glass. The floor is waxed and polished to the last degree, and just before the bed is a small square of carpet, and one will do well to beware of a misstep, so slippery is the floor. In such an inn as this one is treated as an honored guest, and on the day of departure takes his leave often with a real regret.

Contrast this charming picture with that of our own country hotels.

Of course the faultfinder abroad will find food for faultfinding. But most things abroad are well done, and many things are certainly done better than we do them.

ALTKIRCH

Sterne, in his "Sentimental Journey," wrote: "The learned Smelfungus travelled from Boulogne to Paris, from Paris to Rome, and so on; but he set out with spleen and jaundice, and every object he passed by was discolored or distorted. He wrote an account of them; but 'twas nothing but the account of his own miserable feelings."

Let me picture here the day of our own departure from this charming spot, when the swinging door of the old yellow-bodied carriage closed upon us and our impedimenta. The ambling fat mare waving her expressive ears excitedly because of the children gathered to bid us good-by; with Jan on the front seat leaning forward persuasively, holding the reins in both his great red hands, and the old curé waving his shovel hat and shouting to the children: "Allons! mes enfants—Heep!"

A faint response from the children: *"Heep!"* Their eyes are on the carriage, likewise their attention, because of the generous handful of copper coins with which Lady Anne is ready to shower them.

"Allons! encore! plus fort! Heep!"

A still smaller response.

"Allons! mes enfants! Comme un coup de tonnerre, hourah!"

"Bon voyage, Monsieur et Madame," from all the children, but the "Hourah" was not uttered, although it had been so well rehearsed by all of them. They surrounded the old yellow-bodied carriage which was to take us to the station, thrusting little brown hands filled with fresh flowers from the village gardens into Lady Anne's lap. Then followed the shower of copper coins amid the shrill cries of the scrambling youngsters.

"Attention," from the Curé.

They all stand up obediently and in place, the girls on one side, the boys on the other, and the Curé standing in the middle with his hat raised. Down it goes, and at the signal they sing a familiar tune, but what words are these? To our amazed ears came:

—"Goat shave de gracieuse Kveene,
Longue leef de glorieuse Kveene—
Goat shave de Kveene!"

It was all in honor of Lady Anne, and her shining eyes showed that she well appreciated it.

"Now, then, my children," said the Curé, "all attention, eyes front on my hat, all ready. 'Heep! Heep! Hourah!—and Au revoir." This time the children responded courageously.

Jan snapped the whip over the back of the fat mare,

who jumped forward. And thus we passed into the shadows beneath the great trees on the winding, dusty road to the station.

The Feast of the Pipers

The Feast of the Pipers

(LES MÉNÉTRIERS)

THERE is perhaps no Fête day in all of Alsace-Lorraine so well loved by the people as that celebrated yearly as "Pfeiffertag." One of the earliest, if not the very oldest feast days of the Province, it had its origin in the little town of Ribeauville; some say, however, that it was at Ville or Schlestadt that it originated, at any rate during the sixteenth century it had a great vogue at Ribeauville (locally called Rapperschwier), a small town of about 5,000 inhabitants, surrounded by the remains of high stone walls of the fourteenth century, lying at the entrance of a lovely valley, with a winding river, the Strengbach, and many fruitful vineyards. This town is said to have been the very headquarters of The Guild Corporations. For instance, before the Revolution no one could practice any trade or do any work whatever within the limits of the town, without having first been admitted to membership in the Guild governing his craft. Thus a painter or leather worker must have been regularly apprenticed under a known master workman; when, after a period, he must produce a piece of work which, accepted and approved by his master, gave him the right to apply for admission to the Guild. This was the law, and was rigidly enforced. These Guilds included sometimes simply the workers of a town; sometimes those of a whole district. So the musicians of Alsace from the Vosges to the Rhine, and from Bâle to the great Forest of Haguenare, the limits of the ancient Province, were united in one great and powerful corporation, which lasted for four centuries, up to the year 1789. This corporation was known as the Guild of the "Pfeiffers," and these acknowledged members officiated at all dances, fêtes and weddings known as "Kilbes" or "Mestigs" in the strange tongue of the inhabitants.

According to an old law the men of the "Maréchausée" (Marshals of France) and the members of the Corps of Gensd'armes, were bound to learn to play either a flute or a trumpet, and upon proving their skill upon one or both of these instruments were given a certificate and entered upon the records of the corporation. Should any fail in or ignore this, a heavy penalty was inflicted. They enjoyed the protection of the Emperor, who granted them as "fief" to the Seigneur of Ribeaupierre. Thus this Seigneur, who possessed the three great Châteaux of Ribeaupierre, Giersberg and Saint Ulrich, became the King of the Musicians of Alsace, and was known as the "Pfeiffer Köenig," who, however, for various reasons, delegated his powers to a viceroy, who could play the ancient instrument called the "Violé," and who on state occasions wore the crown of the Seigneur and enjoyed temporary powers. The Association included four masters and twelve jurors, who formed the tribune of the corporation, with power to punish those who were brought before them for infractions of any of the rules.

The Count of Rappoltstein was the "King" of all musicians and minstrels of the Upper Rhine up to the year 1673, when he died. The whole brotherhood recognised his authority, and paid him a large yearly tax for the benefit of his protection. The corporation was also a religious association. According to the records, one Eggenolf, a Seigneur of Ribeaupierre, was a crusader and was present at the sacking of Constantinople. He brought home with him an image of the Virgin Mary, which he placed in the chapel of Dusenbach, and this statue was carried in the processions of the Brotherhood. Each member received a medal stamped with the image which he wore on his breast.

On the day of the Fête, the 8th of September, the day of Ménétriers (fiddlers), or "Pfeiffertag," when the small square of the town was filled at early dawn with a motley horde of wandering merchants and their gaily painted wagons; with tumblers and jugglers, and peasants in holiday costumes from the whole country round —from Colmar and Strassburg and even towns farther away, such as Bâle and Wissembourg, the bells in the churches rang loudly, calling upon the musicians to form in line, as if this were necessary. They were already there in all their regalia, with their great corporation banner hung with wreaths of flowers and dangling medals. At the head stood the "Pfeiffer Köenig," clad in royal velvet robes, a crowned head for the occasion, and as proud and haughty as any real monarch. There were more than twenty men carrying the quaint beribboned bagpipes, and an equal number who bore large polished brass horns, some of them trombones. The King carried an ancient "Viole," something in shape like a guitar, and there were several other strangely shaped archaic instruments played with a bow, and held beneath the chin like a violin. The scene was animated and most amusing, but the landlord of the inn, a most doleful individual, regarded it all from his doorway with uplifted eyebrows, and refused to be impressed with it. "Ah," said he, "'Tis not what it was, 'tis nothing nowadays—you should have seen it as I have often seen it when a boy. Then it was something like! This"—contemptuously—"this is nothing—very poor—very poor!—and these men are nothing to-day. In old times they would be the best men of the town, but now they are a poor lot, simply the peasants, M'sieur and Madame, simply the peasants!"

But one could hardly agree with him. It was all most

picturesque to our eyes, and during the whole day and far into the night the musicians played, the tumblers tumbled, and the peasants thronged the streets joyously. There was much eating and a great deal of drinking, of course, but it was all most orderly, and the quaintly clad "gend'arme" had little to do except parade solemnly and look important.

The long street of the little town contains many fine houses of the fifteenth and sixteenth centuries in very good repair.   The fine old tower in the market place is the "Metzgerthurm," a remnant of the ancient fortifications, and there is too a fine "Rathaus," containing a large collection of very beautiful old goblets of repoussé silver, kept in a state of high polish.

The fountain in the square is dated 1536, and farther on is the Gothic parish church, which was completed in the year 1782.   There are the imposing ruins of three great castles here, the Giersberg, built in the thirteenth century and boldly perched on the crest of a precipitous cliff, from which a wonderful view of the Rhine valley is had, and farther on, the very remarkable Saint Ulrichsburg, which is the most modern of the three castles, and was blown up during the Thirty Years' War.   The type of architecture is perhaps the most artistic in this region, if one may make use of the term for want of a better one to qualify it.   The Knights' Hall, a most impressive and spacious room lighted by double windows, is surrounded by niches which once held statues of the Knights. Great flocks of rooks flew in and out of these windows and seemed quite fearless of our presence. The third castle is that of Hoh-Rappoltstein, with a lofty tower, from the summit of which, could one climb it, a most wonderful view must be had, but the stones of the staircase had so fallen away in places that it was evidently dangerous. The country abounds with vineyards, in which the peasantry labor contentedly, and the wine made here is most excellent and astonishingly cheap. Hereabouts are countless small towns of a thousand or two population, each with ruined castles, old walls and bastions and ancient remains too numerous even to mention, and each with most delightful and cleanly inns, where the traveller may sojourn "the world forgetting, by the world forgot," at the cost of five or six francs a day, with pension rates proportionately reduced. Indeed, we had difficulty in leaving Ribeauville (or Rappoltsweiler or Rapperschwier, as it is called indiscriminately by the natives, according to their several preferences), which for two or three days in the year awakes to the drone of the bagpipes, and the delighted dancing of the peasants on the anniversary of the "Pfeiffertag."

As a rule, away from the large cities and towns, especially those nearest to the former German border line, the important meal occurs at two or half past two in the afternoon. I was accustomed to this when I was here in my student days, but it may be imagined that her first dinner in Alsace-Lorraine made an impression upon Lady Anne. The table d'hôte was half filled when we entered the room, the side tables covered with a disorderly array of piled-up dishes, canes, umbrellas, and hats. The buxom, red cheeked, pretty girls in waiting and the fat calm of the expressionless landlord, throned in state at the end of the board, all had an odd look to her. There were already seated a couple of fat Majors, a fat Colonel, and three fat Lieutenants, in full uniform, all of them wearing glittering orders. There was also an officer of higher grade, all grizzled and obese, from whose broad beribboned breast swung a number of medals, stars, and crosses, and from whose naturally grim visage a sabre cut, beginning at the left temple and passing through the upper lip, had removed no iota of natural grimness. On the opposite side of the table were two plump, blue eyed, flaxen haired, good natured looking German ladies, between whom was a little withered fig of an official, whose name, as we caught it, was of but one syllable, but whose title rejoiced in thirteen: "Herr Koniglicher-hoch-ober-teuer-Inspektor Seip!" When he stood up after dinner he appeared about four feet two inches, or possibly two and a half inches, tall, the two and a half inches being boot heel.

His self-importance, however, was immeasurable and most amusing to contemplate. The ladies conversed with him adoringly, and he was all affability and condescension with them, but the officers preserved a solemn silence, eyeing us with some curiosity, I thought. Some of them broke and munched their bread crusts, disordering the space before them; one bored holes in the cloth with the tines of his fork, to the dismay of the red cheeked serving maid who stood behind him. The others had tucked the large, damp linen napkins under their chins, and glanced from time to time impatiently towards the kitchen. The rich odor of soup floated out to us all at once, as the door opened, and it seemed as if all at the table swayed to its subtle flavor with one common impulse, and the hand of each officer moved automatically towards the spoon beside his plate. The H. K. H. O. T. I. Seip emitted a long-drawn "A-h-h," and clapped his diminutive withered hands as the red cheeked maid placed the large, deep soup dish before him, and then, without waiting for the others to be served, fell manfully to work.

Late comers, on entering, wished the feeders "guten appetit" (for these at the table d'hôte on this occasion were all Germans), and they growled and gurgled their responses into the bowls of their spoons. Lady Anne was surprised that the roast beef, which promptly followed the soup, should taste sour, and was disinclined to eat it until I explained the reason and called her attention to the satisfaction upon the part of the other guests, telling her that here in some of these small places where the cooking was in German style, "all is vinegary that is not greasy, and greasy that is not sour." Lady Anne was not prepared to see fish follow roast, nor pastry and marmalade succeed the fish; nor the huge joints of roasted pork and veal that followed the pastry; nor yet the chickens that displaced the roast, to make room in turn for a course of crayfish, and finally the goose quill toothpicks passed in a tall glass from one to the other, and industriously used as a matter of course. All at the table ate heartily of all the dishes, and some sighed as the toothpicks appeared.

By the time the dinner was half over, one heard an occasional remark, but when the crayfish was served a general buzz of conversation ensued, through which rumbled an occasional ponderous chuckleborn German pleasantry. And thus the dinner progressed and ended.

As a mark of courtesy, we were invited to a christening celebration in the village, to be exact, at the edge of the village, Burgomeister Kugelspiel and Frau Burgomeisterinn Kugelspiel and the two plump flaxen haired maidens who were pledges of their affection; and the maid who carried the iron lantern with which to light us on our way home, escorted us.

There we found a large gathering, more majors and young lieutenants in spick and span uniforms and embryo mustaches; a dozen young girls, and stout mamas and papas of greater or less obesity, all bent evidently upon having a very "deuce" of a time. Most of the men smoked long stemmed pipes with elaborately decorated and betasseled china bowls, except the officers, who smoked only black cigars.

There was a great deal of eating and drinking, the ladies sipping black coffee, and consuming pounds and pounds of heavy sweet cake, while the men ate cold meats and such, washing it down with copious and frequent drafts of Rhenish wine, all with that enormous and remarkable power of deglutition confined alone to German burghers.

And thus having eaten, drunk and smoked, they were all in great good humor, smiling fat expressive smiles of calm joy in existence. Therefore there was nothing left but black coffee, the inevitable glass of brandy, and the contemplative pipe.

In the drawing room, young people waltzed and polka'd, accompanied by a piano and violin, while in the corners the plump, placid mamas played whist or gossiped.

Out in the garden we found the young mother exhibiting the baby with pride. Afterwards we saw her executing a slow waltz with the happy father, in which she revolved with true bovine gracefulness towards the dining room, and our last-view of them both through the open window as we departed, showed her pressing tenderly upon his acceptance a gigantic cut of sausage.

When he put it to his lips her heart quite melted within her, and as she sank upon his bosom overcome with joy and tenderness, she exclaimed: "O thou dearest and most blessed man!"

"They are so happy," said the Frau Burgomeisterinn Kugelspiel to Lady Anne. "Ach!—is it not beautiful to behold?"

Mulhouse

Mulhouse

ALTHOUGH Mulhouse [1] is a very old town, excepting the restored, quaintly gabled, be-statued and gilded Hôtel de Ville, there is little to attract the antiquary. Mulhouse is to-day an intensely modern town—at least in the estimation of the Mulhousians. There was formerly in the center of the town an old church, the temple of Saint Étienne, built in the twelfth century, with a choir and steeple of the fourteenth century, but this was demolished in 1858, and a vast construction in doubtful taste was erected upon the site. However, a fine tower called the "Bollwerk," which formed part of the ancient fortifications of Mulhouse, yet stands, and is kept in excellent repair. The Mulhousians exhibit it with some pride, too, but one can well see that the inhabitants are not busied with, or interested in, the past. There are indeed some rather pathetic imitations of what they call modernity. But the people are modest to a fault, and kindly to the last degree. The little river, the Doller, is the fortune of the town. Evil smelling as it is, its quality is valued highly in the bleacheries, and more especially as applied to colors and

1 Mulhouse: The French form of the name.

dyes, and of this river they are very proud. If you ask them leading questions concerning art and architecture they exhibit some surprise mingled with annoyance, and again point to the Town Hall. So one returns to it for a second examination.

The building is the sole survival of the ancient type which occupied the square when this whole district was destroyed by a conflagration in the sixteenth century. In the detail of its lines, and in spite of its many restorations it has very well preserved its ancient character, and its ogival portal with baldaquin and columns marks the period between the end of the Gothic and beginning of the Renaissance. Montaigne, who visited Mulhouse in the year 1580, made the following enthusiastic entry in his diary: "The Hôtel de Ville at Mulhouse; a magnificent palace, all statues, painting and gilding." The paintings on the outside walls, frequently restored, are still to be seen, and represent Mercy, Truth, Prudence, Temperance, Faith, Hope and Charity. These figures decorate the whole front of the edifice, and furnish all the art that Mulhouse needs or can stand, apparently, at least since the Prussians seized the province.

On one of the lateral façades a curiosity is pointed out to the stranger with various explanations. It represents a human head suspended by a chain before a tablet containing an inscription setting forth that all "Bavards" (prattlers) and "Médisants" (slanderers) were condemned to carry this mask suspended about their necks,[1] and thus expose themselves in the market place on market days according to their sentences. This object is called the "Klapperstein." And the people gravely explain to the stranger that "Of course it is not used nowadays!"

The life of Mulhouse, which might perhaps get upon one's nerves had one to dwell there for a length of time, is for a short sojourn sufficiently amusing. The café life is modeled upon that of Paris, although the signs are all in German, and the "consommation" is the same as that in France. The beer served is very good, and the places where it is sold are quite crowded by prosperous looking men with their wives and daughters. The town is one of the most ancient in Europe, but aims to be most modern. It is famous for the construction in 1839 of a railway line by Nicolas Koechlin, a citizen of Mulhouse, from this city to Thann, at a time when such enterprises were looked upon as sheer lunacy. The inhabitants are vastly proud of the "new quarter," as it is called, where there are wide avenues constructed upon a uniform plan, with large and imposing-looking houses built with ar-

[1] On the plaque is the following:

"Zum Klapperstein bin ich genannt
Den böken Mäutern wohf bekannt
Mer Lust zu zant und hader hat
Der mus mich tragen durch die Stadt."

cades about a space shaped like a fan. It would seem as if the whole population of ninety-one thousand passes through this quarter daily, especially along the resplendent Rue du Sauvage (The Wildmangasse, as the Prussians have insisted upon naming it). This street is famed all over Alsace as at once the great business street and promenade, and here one can study the manners and customs, as well as the dialects, so difficult for the tourist to understand.

Mulhouse is a great center for Societies, and these are subdivided into innumerable "Comités." At the head is the great "Société Industrielle," formed in 1825 by a group of twenty-two citizens of Mulhouse. This now comprises the "Comités" of Chemistry, Machinery, Commerce, History and Statistics, Natural History, Fine Arts, and Public Utility. These bring forth practical ideas for the public welfare, which most enthusiastically have been adopted by the authorities. As, for instance, the Artisans' Colony (Arbeiter Stadt), a large tract in the northwestern part of the town, purchased in 1853 by Mayor Jean Dollfus, and presented by wealthy citizens to the town. This was one of the earliest attempts to provide good and cheap houses for the working classes. It is said to have been successful for a number of years, but is now occupied by a somewhat higher class of tenants than formerly.

The wide canal of the Rhone and the Rhine bordered

by spacious quays, and lined with modern château-like buildings, is very attractive and impressive, and there is a new Post Office at the draw-bridge, over which the people are genuinely enthusiastic. In the face of all this newness and splendor the voice of the antiquary is hushed, and either the heavy smoke of the manufactories or the fine, clean promenade of the Tannenwald, from which all the old towers and walls have been torn down and carted away, have driven him hence. In truth, one must admit that Mulhouse came late to France, and only remained French for less than seventy-five years, but certainly she gave to France all her heart as well as all of her economic interests. When the separation of 1871 came, there seemed an end of all hope for Mulhouse, and many of the merchants and millers left the province and re-established themselves and their mills across the frontier, for example, at Epinal and at Belfort. Perhaps more than any other Alsatian town, Mulhouse has preserved its attachment for France, and especially for Paris, which it so comically imitates. If they think that you are a trustworthy confidant, Mulhousians will tell you many interesting things about the Prussians, some of which will shock you more or less, depending upon just how familiar you may be with Prussian customs throughout Alsace; but these details can have no place in this chronicle.

But one fact may be stated here which is surprising.

ALSACE-LORRAINE

The Prussians do not feel comfortable in Mulhouse, for there are less than ten thousand of them there, not ten per cent. of the population, and this in spite of the fact that Mulhouse is one of the richest in natural resources of all the towns of Alsace-Lorraine. Then, too, it is to be remarked that the Kaiser, in all his visits to the Province, has never once visited Mulhouse. There must be a very potent reason for this omission.

Wandering about the old part of the town, one came upon a section of ancient wall at an angle of which was a most delightful and satisfying tall tower of slender proportions, surmounted by a steep pent roof, all gayly "flèched," and furnished with a pointed window of charming character. The upper part of the tower was white-washed, and below this section was a large and very well executed mural decoration, representing a knight "cap-a-pie" on horseback before a background of walled town, all set forth with blue, orange, and crimson and gold in most artistic fashion. The tower joined two sections of wall pierced by wide arched gates, and here the narrow street was lined with closed and shuttered small two and three storied houses, the doors of which had large brass knobs and handles. I loitered about this gateway tower for nearly twenty minutes, and during this time not a soul passed save an old woman with a basket of eels, who either would not, nor could not, understand my questions. All she would say was, "Bollwerk—Bollwerk—M'sieur"—so I had to give it up, but I made a sketch of the tower and the gateway. From a little book published in Mulhouse I gathered the following facts: "The town of Mulhouse owes its birth to a mill built upon the banks of the river Ill, at the entrance of the great plain of Alsace, and almost at equal distance from the Rhine and the Vosges. During the Middle Ages it formed a part of the League of the Ten Imperial Cities of Alsace, but in the sixteenth century it joined the Helvetian Cantons and adopted, like Berne, the Protestant religion. Its independence was maintained in 1648, and Mulhouse became part of French territory. In the eighteenth century the town, hitherto agricultural, became industrial. Great merchants such as Schmalzer, Koechlin, and Dollfus built mills to carry on the manufacture of cotton and dyes, which attracted an army of workmen. Thus the products of Mulhouse became celebrated in all the markets of the world, and the towns were enriched. At the time of the Revolution France established custom houses on the banks of the Rhine, so Mulhouse could not send any of her products over into Germany or Switzerland, in consequence of which and partly from an attraction of sentiment—"raisons de la cœur"—she resolved to join with France. So on the 3rd of January, 1798, those at the head of the little Republic voted for reunion with the Republic of France by 97 votes against 15. The treaty of reunion was signed and the fête of celebration was fixed for March 15th, with Metzer, deputy of the Upper Rhine, at the head of the delegates. On the appointed day and amid salvos of artillery the event was solemnized. A great number of triumphal arches of liberty were erected in various quarters of the town, which was decked with flags. A fine procession composed of the ancient magistrates paraded the principal streets. There were also cortèges of Mulhousians in ancient costume, and young girls bearing a large banner of white satin upon which was a patriotic inscription, followed by a lady in rich costume carrying a white satin cushion on which lay a scroll manuscript of the French constitution. These cortèges proceeded to the "Grande Place," where tribunes had been prepared; one by the magistrates of Mulhouse, the other by the French authorities. Metzger, addressing his allocution to the Ancient Council of Mulhouse, demanded to know if there was any act of sovereignty which he was desired to accomplish. In response, the magistrates delivered to the Council of Illzach all their duties against Mulhouse, and then handed over the letters of enfranchisement. The magistrate then read the treaty of reunion aloud, and amid salvos from the cannon in the "Grande Place," the French municipality was installed. From this day on Mulhouse was a French town, but also, it must be said, she maintained a certain individuality. The children of the citizens were educated to become

merchants, millers and dyers. Mulhouse remained a city of free initiatives. Its inhabitants, without demanding any help from the State, created great schools, in which were taught spinning, weaving, chemistry, including courses for young girls. A great industrial and social community was built and endowed, and Mulhouse prospered.—Then came the Franco-Prussian War.

. . . If one wishes, it is possible to be free of the bondage of railway travel in Alsace, for everywhere at low rates one can obtain delightfully comfortable old carriages at low rates, and quaintly garbed drivers, who gladly entertain one with folk lore of more or less truthful quality. One may thus be restored to the romance of travel such as our posting grandparents enjoyed. There is to be had thus the delight of taking a town unawares, so to speak, "stealing upon it by back ways and unchronicled paths," and discovering in it, perchance, an aspect hidden away by the bulk of some railway embankment or the ugly brick wall of a station.

It is a most delightful country, this Alsace-Lorraine. "land of mountain ways—dear haunted land of gorge and glen," broken by waves of vine-clad hill, and fertile well watered valley; and dotted with the villages, and frequent, smiling, happily located villages, with well paved, quaintly shaped market places surrounded by archaic arcaded houses on which unmolested long legged storks build their ragged nests and rear their young,

ALSACE-LORRAINE

The country is green in summer, so full and close in texture, so pleasantly diversified by clumps of dark woodland in the valleys, and by those silvery, mill-embossed streams threading the fields with light; all has the added beauty of reach and amplitude. There is constant charm of detail in all these small towns thus reached in the leisurely drawn old carriage through which we thus passed with perfect content and confidence in the ability of the fat old white hollow-backed horse, which ambled along with head on one side, regarding us solemnly from one sympathetic, limpid and understanding eye, and in the stream of folk-lore, more or less gratuitously supplied by our driver. The landscape opens and closes in endless variety, and the villages, some of them perched high upon ridges, with old houses stumbling down at most picturesque angles, and others tucked away in dim, misty hollows among thick orchards, with all the pleasant country industries reaching often up to the open doors of the old towered churches. In many of the smaller villages thus come upon, deep pent roofs overhang the plastered and beamed walls of the cottages, all "espaliered" with crab apple and pear trees, and lines of quacking ducks swim in ordered rows in the ponds, so well fringed with hawthorn and laburnum. There is always some note of distinction to be met with; here the arched gateway of a sixteenth century château; there the mossy wall of a triple-arched abbey, or church, or ancient guild hall.

Everything about this rich, juicy land is bathed in a tender, lambent light unlike any other that I have met with; it is characteristically Alsatian, even to the round, red cheeks of the strangely clad children, and the drowsy grouping of the fat sleek cattle in lush pastures. It is all cultivated and disciplined to the very last point of finish, this expanse of hill and plain and valley, and proves how nature may be utilized to the last degree without losing an iota of its naturalness and charm. In some regions of this much coveted country, where space is restricted, the endless walls and lines of fruit trees bordering the straight roads may weary one, but as a rule here in Alsace, where cultivation is hand in hand with all unconscious sentiment, one finds the higher beauty of the land developed, bespeaking long familiar intercourse between the soil and the inhabitants, where almost every field has a place in history and a name, and each guarded tree a feudal designation. And so on we jogged along the curved level road which bordered the river Lauch, tributary of the Ill and the Logelbach, toward the town of Colmar, in no hurry to reach it, be it understood, for this was a journey of leisure as well as sentiment.

We continually checked the jogging pace of the fat old white horse to enjoy the bright gardens on the banks, and the green promontories reflected on the surface of the stream. The many old castles and manors of brown or gray stone, over-topping the dense thickets of lilac and laburnum, and on the river reaches, where old slouch-hatted and red-vested fishermen nodded over their poles, till in the distance we saw the crests of the dim mountains, which are only two miles or so from Colmar.

Colmar

Colmar

EAVING the attractive cross-country road, here and there embowered by large trees bordering the fertile farm lands, we turned into a wide, well-paved avenue, which at length was continuously lined by rows of neat white modern-looking houses of stucco, but of no particular character or interest. This avenue led through the Public Garden to the Grande Place, or "Champs de Mars," which seemed well nigh deserted, save for a few sleepy coachmen lolling upon the seats of some archaic-looking cabs, patiently waiting for fares. Past the bronze monument to the great Admiral Bruat by the sculptor Bartholdi, who modeled our Statue of Liberty in the harbor of New York, and turning the corner all at once we were in the midst of the bustle of a busy city. There were lines of street peddlers with barrows noisily calling out their wares; trolley cars with clanging gongs and grinding, creaking wheels, all laden with people; long lines of workmen liberated for the noon hour from the factories thronged the sidewalks, and before the numerous cafés prosperous-looking people sat at small iron tables, drinking and smoking. Threading the Rufachers Strasse, we passed with some difficulty through the thronging multitude into the Kleber Strasse, and so on to the ancient inner town, in great contrast to the modernity of the other and newer part. There we found narrow, picturesque streets and byways, and buildings of the sixteenth and seventeenth centuries grouped about the old cruciform Gothic church of St. Martin. Here were dim shady ways, lined with ancient houses painted in faded tones of rose and green, with tiled roofs hidden by the leafy branches of tall trees in the courtyards.

Always these old towns grew up around the great churches, and perhaps nowhere is this fact brought home to one more clearly than in Colmar. If St. Martin's Church has not the splendors of Strassburg Cathedral to offer, it certainly is a notable example of the ogival period in Alsace, and occupies the first rank among the sacred edifices of the Province. Of course, as may be imagined and expected, it suffered greatly during the Reformation; its precious glass was destroyed, its sacristy pillaged, and its chime of bells carried off. The Revolution demolished its carved stalls and altars, and the splendid oaken confessionals were broken up and sold for kindling wood. The Revolutionaries, so we are told, placed statues of Voltaire and Rousseau in the nave, and exalted the "God of Reason" in the temple from whose summit "shone a great bonfire in an iron basin, visible for miles around."

Near at hand is a small square in which is the Dominican Church of the thirteenth century. Here was silence and shadows; old high walled houses with lace-adorned windows; old walls of mellowed brick, pierced by mysterious low, small doors painted green, and adorned with highly polished and inviting brass knockers. Here old cloaked women, lace-capped, stopped to gossip in the shadows, while overhead in the sunlight doves flew about the cornices and gables. One heard the distant rumbling notes of a great organ, punctuated by the laughter and cries of children playing somewhere behind the walls. The ancient Place aux Recollets contains the celebrated "Arcades," the habitation of the Protestant pastors. It is a good example of seventeenth century construction, so architects say—with pointed turrets, and festooned gable.

Near it is the "Douane," or custom house, belonging to a more ancient period, some say the fifteenth century. Its history covers a multitude of uses, and at one time, in the eighteenth century it served as Hôtel de Ville. Today it is used as a museum of antiquities. It is remarkable for two different styles of architecture, the most ancient of which offers, with its beautiful balustrade, so fine and so simple in design, a most precious example of the Gothic art of the end of the fifteenth century in

Alsace. Colmar is indeed rich in ancient halls and houses. The list is too long to include in one chapter. There is the so-called "Maison des Têtes," of the purest Renaissance, celebrated for its embellishment of masks and grimacing heads which ornament the columns of the windows, the two balconies of the tourelle, and the portal. There is the Maison Pfister, formerly the Sign of the Chapeau, of the date 1537, perhaps the most curious in all Alsace, with its quaint wooden gallery, its "cage d'escalier," or staircase, and its "encore" belled tower ornamented, gilded, and frescoed wth religious paintings. There are also the Maison Macker, late Gothic period; the Vaisseau d'Or, of the sixteenth century; the Renaissance portal of the Maison Hillenmeyer, and, the Maison Adolph, all meriting detailed description, and of undoubted character.

Many of the houses of Colmar bear emblazoned inscriptions on their fronts in old Latin or ornate German —as, for example, "Deus dedit incrementum, Deus quoque custodiet," says one. "Pax intrantibus, salus exeuntibus," says another. "Accrescat domui res simul et decus, egregiis factis debita gloria," and "Soli Deo gloria." Then in the old German: "Ehe veracht als gemacht" (Easier to criticise than to execute). "Fide, sed vide, drau aber schau wem" (Beware in whom thou confidest). "Der Gott vertraut, ist wohl gebaut" (Who so confides in God is well built). "Ich baue für mich, sih du für dich" (I build for myself, look out for thyself). Generally when there is no inscription over the door, it will be found on the lintel, or there will be some sort of shield or escutcheon bearing the arms or the emblem of the householder; or again, the house will be named for some object, flower or animal. Thus one finds the house of the Bear, the house of the Rose, or that of the Lily, each with its painted or sculptured emblem.

In the little street of the Augustans is pointed out the house in which Martin Schongauer, the painter, was born, and where the great Voltaire lived and labored over his "Annals of the Empire" in 1753. Here dwelt the powerful Society of the Corporations, a body composed of the governing heads of the various trades of the province. Superficial as was of course our view of the old town, Colmar seemed all sufficient unto herself. Behind the small panes of their shop windows the merchants seemed to wait for customers without any visible impatience, much as their ancestors must have done in days long gone. Movements in the streets were unhurried. People gossiped in the open doors. The costumes of the peasants seemed to be of the same cut as that in the old prints, as far as we could judge. We were told that many of the younger people went over the border into France after the annexation, rather than live under German rule, but I must confess that there seemed to be plenty of young people in the town during the days we spent there.

There were certainly a great many German soldiers in uniform everywhere, and many times I heard them conversing in French in the cafés where they gathered. I confess that I was surprised at this, for I had been told that the use of the French tongue was forbidden to the soldiers in Alsace. But when I asked the proprietor of the café about it, he only shrugged his shoulders, and with uplifted eyebrows exclaimed enigmatically: "It is forbidden to give information against the Government."

But certainly I heard the French tongue in use at Colmar quite as much as the German. Behind the museum, where the old people congregated, at the base of the Statue of the poet Pfeffel, in the crowded center of the town; on the banks of the river where the washwomen were at work in long lines, their voices and their laughter heard above the noise of their paddles so deftly wielded, I heard French spoken without any attempt at concealment. Likewise in the somewhat grimy dining room of the "Schwarzes-Lamm" in the Rapp Platz, where we had a culminating surprise in the excellence of the table d'hôte, and where amid the onion-scented gathering at the long, clean table the people grouped cheerfully, while a flushed-faced buxom handmaiden laid before us a remarkable succession of the most varied and well-cooked dishes. There was a tender filet, an airy soufflé, some delicious artichokes with butter sauce, and coffee that was fragrant and real. Here in this small hostelry of the sign of the Black Lamb, with the German flag flying over the door and two German officers at the end of the long table, the only ones who spoke German were the landlord and the flush-faced handmaiden who passed the viands. The officers addressed us quite civilly, when they found that we were Americans, and not English, as they had fancied, asking if we had seen the great Saint Martin's Church, and if we did not greatly admire the fifteenth century stained glass? One, the younger, and a handsome blond giant of a fellow disclosed the fact that he had been an art student in Berlin, and was able to criticise intelligently the painting by Martin Schongauer in the Sacristy, "The Madonna in an Arbor of Roses." He spoke of the retouching of the painting as adding harshness to the already harsh manner of the painter. It was he who directed us to the old abbey church, containing a remarkable collection of early German paintings, where works of Mathias Grunewald (1529), the chief Rhenish painter, were to be seen. It was here that Bartholdi was born and lived before he went to Paris to study sculpture. The young officer knew all about this, but modestly said that he had never had the honor of meeting Bartholdi. He thereafter discoursed learnedly with Lady Anne, concerning the early

German School of painting, mentioning too quite casually the fact that Erwin of Steinbach was the originator of Strassburg Minster, and insisting that the details of the Gothic architecture were no mere slavish copying of existing examples. We were both surprised at his learning, as well as his modest bearing, which was quite at variance with what we had been led to expect. Afterwards, when the meal was over and most of the gathering had departed, including the two officers, our host informed us that the young officer was a nobleman, a "Hochzeit."

The next day we had the pleasure of riding out to a small town, Eguisheim, where the fête called "Le Mestig" in Alsace takes place every year. Here there is a very badly restored palace (called "Pfalz") of the eighth century, and an old castle called the Dreien-Eguisheim, with three great stone towers visible for miles around. These towers are known severally as the "Dagsburg," the "Wahlenburg," and the "Wekmund," and collectively as the "Drei Exen." Like all fêtes in Alsace, this "Mestig," so called, began with a banquet at the inn, and, we were told, one in almost every large household. At the inn table, which was crowded, we had difficulty in getting seats, but at length room for us was good-humoredly made by the already crowded holiday folk. There was noodle soup in plenty, which was noisily consumed, rabbit and hare stuffed with pudding, and an enormous roast of pork, which was carved by mine host at a side table. There were many family reunions, and cousins and friends of the villages kissed and embraced each other in unaffected heartiness. Many of the villagers wore archaic and amusing costumes, were generally burdened with large baskets, and the elders were armed with large horn-handled umbrellas of various faded tones of green and brown cotton, evidently treasured heirlooms. Advantageously placed at the windows of the second floor front salon of the inn, which overlooked the small "place d'armes," we watched the preparations at ease. It is said that officially no fête can begin until the gendarme gives the word. That word cannot be given, understand, until he is satisfied by examination that the German flag is properly displayed according to the law as set forth in his little glazed black oilcloth-covered manual, which he carries in his belt. That German flag, he must see personally, is to be hoisted to its place above all others. He must see to it, too, that no tri-color of France is visible anywhere. He must assure himself that no toy balloons bearing the prescribed tri-color are on sale at any booth, nor must there be any gingerbread cakes bearing the blue, white and red colors of France exposed for sale during the fête. It may seem incredible to the tourist, but Germany was said to be in great danger, and should any of these rules be ignored no one knows what would happen. The danger is, that in spite of the great line of forts armed with monster Krupp cannon, which guard Alsace-Lorraine from France; in spite of the hundreds of thousands of German soldiers that occupy the lost provinces, should any of these rules be disregarded by the gendarme who is stalking solemnly from booth to booth in the square under our eyes, in performance of his duty to the Fatherland, the country might be lost to Germany—so untrustworthy were these people! And all through the act of one small boy blowing a blast on a small gingerbread whistle bearing the surreptitiously blazoned tricolor in blue, red and white sugar!

But the gendarme finds all in order, and gives the word to the leader of the town band, who is most anxiously awaiting it. This band of eight, carrying severally a bass drum; a snare ditto; a large brass (battered) horn; a trombone ditto; a fife; a bagpipe; a cornet, and a chime of bells on a pole, preceded a long procession of personages in archaic costume, each wearing upon the breast of his long-tailed black frock coat several medals dangling from red and green ribbons. These were followed by some men who, we were told, were to wrestle for prizes given by the authorities each year.

Upon the steps of the town hall stood M. the Mayor in a tall silk hat and full evening dress, wearing his sash of office across his breast. To him proceeded a young girl dressed all in white and wearing a beribboned headdress. With a pretty curtsey, she gave him a cake;

wrapped in scalloped white paper, and received from him a kiss upon each cheek. The leader of the band now raised his baton; there came a blare of sound and rattle of drum, and the fête (or Mestig) was formally pronounced open. The band, vying with each other as to which should make the loudest discord, made a tour of the square. The wrestlers wrestled barefooted on a space railed off near the fountain; the local fire company, in brass helmets and horsehair plumes, dragging an absurd red pump, trundling noisily on four small iron wheels, marched and countermarched beneath our windows until we applauded them; and everyone ate spiced cakes and drank all the wine they could hold, all the afternoon. At night there was to be a grand ball, but we did not stay to see it. This was a real and typical Mestig, so the inn-keeper said, and he added that we "might voyage throughout Alsace-Lorraine and not see one so good," and in truth he was right, we never did.

We were told of another fête which is celebrated in Alsace during the month of January of each year. This is called the fête of the Emperor, and the crown officer of each village vies with the neighboring one as to which shall make the most patriotic display on that occasion. There is, to begin with, it appears, the singing of the Emperor's hymn; then the "Wacht am Rhein," and to finish, a most tiresome discourse, setting forth the virtues and greatness of the Emperor, at the end of which the listeners are expected to shout loudly, "Hoch!" "But," said my informant with a wink, "the little ones have learned to open their mouths wide without making one sound!" This shows how the people love the conquerors —how loyal they are to them, how brave the people, young and old, are in the face of the enemy who occupies their beloved land.

For the Alsatians, the fête they love best is that of the 14th of July— the national fête of their own France. This they celebrate with all their hearts and souls in every hamlet, village, town and city throughout the land —*but in silence*—until they reach the town of Nancy, over the border. On that day, from early dawn, all the roads leading across the frontier are crowded with the faithful, journeying there in all kinds of vehicles, and some even on foot, with one common goal, one purpose in mind, to reach Nancy for the fête. For this they screw and toil and pinch throughout the year, but they consider the money well spent. . . .

But to return to Colmar, with which we were occupied for several days most delightfully.

The town contains many monuments, in which the history of the whole region has been written. The museum, for instance, not because of its pictures, or its treasures of illuminated books, but because of its own artistic glory. This ancient structure, which includes a church, a cloister, and the conventual buildings, was formerly the

Dominican convent, all of the thirteenth century—a vast quadrilateral structure with upright ogival windows. Beside it, the theatre occupies the emplacement of the hostelry.

The convent, the most illustrious among all those in Colmar, is that called the "Unterlinden," built by two pious widows, Agnes de Hergenheim and Agnes de Mittelhelm in 1232. Later it was enlarged and transferred, under the rule of Saint Augustin, and called "Uf Muhlen." After the pillage it passed to the property of Saint Dominique. There were, it seems, eight nuns to inhabit it, all coming from humble families in the neighboring villages. "Very soon," says the chronicle, "their piety, their zeal, the sufferings which they bore, reduced them to docile spirits, to whom were granted visions and ecstasies, which made them famous throughout the land." In the annals of mysticism they held first place. One cannot read without profound emotion the book of Catherine Guebwiller, "Flame of Sanctity," telling how she entered the convent at the tender age of ten, and wrote for seventy years the lives of the first sisters. This manuscript, the original of which is the property of the Library of Bâle, expresses in mystic language the rules of the order, and the letters addressed by the Savant Dom Pitre to Père Lacordaire. And with what enchantment did she evoke the spirit of the life she led there.

"The letters set before us vividly the picture of the

regular promenade held daily by the visionaries as they paced the dim galleries, two by two, now appearing in some chance golden sunbeam, only to vanish among the vines and shadows of the arcade. They were clad in robes of thick white cloth, and wore upon their meekly inclined heads long black veils. They saw visions, these gentle women. Elizabeth of Lennheim 'beheld a great white light' as she prayed, and though ignorant, found afterwards that she could 'read fluently the words of the Bible.' Margaret of Colmar saw, on the day of the Pentecost, as she was chanting the 'Veni Creator,' a dazzling celestial fire burning. Gertrude de Reinfelden and the Lady Adelaide d'Epfig were exhorted on their death beds by an angel. For Agnes de Hergenheim, the songs of birds, the hum of insects, the thousand and one noises of nature, seemed a hymn of praise offered to the Deity. She said: 'To me the blooming rose seems the image of ardent and chaste love, as the lily typifies innocence.' . . . Thus these holy women lived within these cloisters until the Revolution put an end to their visions and ecstasies. The convent was closed, and the sisters scattered. The last of them is said to have died at the age of eighty-seven in 1855. When Père Lacordaire came to Strassburg as preacher he hastened to the bedside of the sister Henriette Spiess, who was even then passing away. 'He wished to behold with his own eyes,' says M.

Paul Acker in his charming chronicle,[1] 'one of these "mystic flowers" whose perfume had embalmed all Christian Europe.'"

These old walls to-day enclose all that is left of the former treasures of the art of Colmar, and the custode was delighted to show us the ancient seats; the portraits of the stolid-looking presidents of the sovereign council; the rusty old battle-axes and halberds, and the battle flags of the town. We were more interested perhaps in the sword of General Rapp, the defender of Dantzig, and the last French flag that flew over Colmar when the Germans violated the place in 1871. The old custode regarded me narrowly as he pointed it out, and when I saluted it, removing my hat, tears rose in his eyes. Brushing them away, he laid his right hand upon his heart, backed away from me, brought his heels together with a click, and saluted with all the manner of a grenadier of the Guard.

In the old parish church we found an admirable painting of the Virgin "Madonna in an Arbor of Roses," and a "terrific" crucifixion by Mathias Grunewald, which was formerly over the great altar of the church of the Antonites at Isenheim. This was the masterpiece of the painter, who was renowned as the chief Rhenish artist painter of the sixteenth century, and who worked mainly

[1] "Colmar," par Paul Acker. Paris.

at Mayence and Aschaffenburg. This painting was the chief treasure of the old abbey church. "Nothing," says an eminent critic, "can surpass the sentiment of horror aroused by the presentment of the 'Great Tragedy.' The livid figure of the Christ against the starring sky; the drooping head; the clenched hands . . . the work of an extraordinary realist and colorist."

There were also numerous panels, the work of Martin Schongauer, he whom the French call "le beau Martin," who was born in Colmar, probably about 1480. It is said that Albert Dürer learned from Schongauer, "who invented it," the art of drawing and engraving on wood. Long after the latter's death, it is said the German artists of the period of the fifteenth and sixteenth centuries copied his mannerisms and his pictures. At any rate, he gave to the town its crown of art in the series of panels in this old church hidden away in Alsace.

Colmar is certainly a most charming spot in which to tarry; each day brought forth some pleasant experience among the people. When one thinks of it, it is as a small corner of earth, fragrant with memories of a glorious past and quite untouched by those modern German architects who have laid profane hands upon well nigh every other town in the province. As it is, it presents an image of great charm and character.

The present writer is conscious of his inability to render in a manner satisfactory to himself his impressions of what he has seen, for the abundance of matter is almost overwhelming after journeying over these lovely winding roads, along the tree bordered streams, each place repeating its charms, "like the successive states of an etched plate," to borrow one of Miss Wharton's artistic similes. The road widens here and there, and as often contracts, leaving the stream now and then to run along beneath frowning crags, beyond which the river again appears coquettishly sparkling behind fringes of old gray willow trees that bend thirstily over it. Long shadows are stealing down the sides of the tree-clad hills, and again the singing river shows, now golden in the sunbeams. Our driver, who had lapsed into silence, now turned round on his seat and pointed with his whip.

"See there, Monsieur and Madame"—he was pointing to an enormous dark, bare rock on the right hand, towering high in the air—"V'là Roche aux Corbeaux." He cracked his whip skilfully and loudly, and a black crowd of crows rose from the rock; there must have been hundreds of the noisy cawing creatures, which careered about for some moments before settling once more on the rock. Our driver looked as if he expected to be rewarded for this entertainment, and "clicked" up the old horse with a smile of triumph. He seemed disappointed and puzzled when we talked of the delicious green of the meadow below with the dancing river, and the banks all purple with early autumn crocus. Here we got out and dallied for a while, climbing the wooded hillside and gathering the rich treasures of Gueldres rose berries of every exquisite tint growing here in fresh beauty.

In a hollow on the left was a half-ruined mill. The cliff rose abruptly behind it, thickly wooded. The mill seemed niched in its dark deserted corner, and a fine white mist that rose from the rushing deep water clung about the thatch of the lonely house. We asked if any one lived there. Our driver shook his head, looking serious. "Ma foi, no," said he, "I should think not, it has been empty since I was a young lad." "What happened to the people?" Lady Anne asked, scenting a story. "Heh, Madame?—Well, he speculated and ruined himself. Then he died, and voilà! his wife died too." He touched up the old horse with the whip and drove along as if he thought that we should be satisfied with this statement, but Lady Anne's interest was not nearly quieted.

"But," said she, "it looks like a good spot for mill business. Why is it empty—why did not some one take it after they died?"

"Ah, bah! so they did, one or two, you understand. But no one stays there, and, you see, it is going fast to ruin. Seems as if a curse was on it."

We looked at one another; there was certainly a ghost at the bottom of this story. "Come now," I said, feel-

136

ingly, "is the mill haunted? Perhaps there is some evil spirit that frightens the people away."

He laughed—a hearty guffaw; then he turned round upon us, giving a keen look to see if I was in earnest. "Ma foi, Monsieur and Madame," he cried, "there may be a ghost for all I know; but if there is, 'tis the ghost called 'lack o' money' that keeps people away from such a tumble-down old place"—and then he busied himself with the reins, and would say no more. But Lady Anne says that she is sure that there is a story connected with the old mill, and that if I had not been so persistent about the matter, had been a trifle less insistent with him, that he might have told us, for the peasant is ever wary of what he calls "*blague*," at the least hint of which he shuts up like the proverbial clam.

The Vineyards

The Vineyards

THE traveler who confines himself to the larger towns rarely becomes familiar with the real characteristics of the people. It is necessary to go out into the country and live for a while among the farmers, who are glad to welcome the stranger, who can assure them that he is willing to conform to their way of living, and so to say "take pot luck." Rarely will he suffer in consequence, be it urged, for the very best in the house is at his command. The beds are clean and good, and the food, though simple, is the same, and all for almost whatever one chooses to pay, while the good-will and hospitality of the farmers of Alsace-Lorraine are proverbial.

Here within a few miles of Colmar is a region filled with interest and charm; of legend and antiquity; and if one is not interested in these, there is the practical side of vine culture, and the gathering and pressing of the grape to be witnessed in all its perfection. The valley of the Rheingau, of course, produces the very finest of the wines, but here in the Sundgau grapes are grown, with which experts are well content. The delicious white

141

wines, pressed from the fragrant grapes grown upon the sunny slopes in the neighborhood, can, in the opinion of experts, successfully compete in quality with any other produced. The great Liebig affirmed that the exquisite bouquet of the white wines is owing to the free acid which they contain, and that certain of their most salutary properties arise from the percentage of tartar present in them. Another great advantage is the almost total absence of brandy, an ingredient invariably found in the wines of Spain and Sicily, which is said to be so injurious both to the flavor of the wine and the health of the drinker. It is said by competent authorities that these so called Rhine wines often retain their bouquet and excellence for a half century, although they rarely contain more than nine per cent. of alcohol. The Still Hoch or the Moselle is wine highly recommended by the people, and is to be had in perfection at the cost of three or four marks a bottle. The Moselle wines are chiefly grown amidst wild rugged fields and sterile seeming slaty rock, and are distinguished by their extraordinarily delicate, aromatic flavor. The best of these are "Berncastler Doctor," "Brauneberger," and "Ohligsberger." These wines are largely consumed in their several districts. The yield is said to be by no means uniformly excellent, for climatic conditions are not the same throughout the region. The vineyards in the most favored positions, where the grapes ripen soonest, often, so it is said, suffer the most severely from the heavy early spring frosts. In a good season, or what the growers call a good "full autumn," rarely attained, a "Morgen," that is, about three-fifths of an acre of land, planted with three or four thousand vines, is expected to yield five "Ohm," or about one hundred and fifty gallons of wine. I had many of these details and technical terms from a little book written by the French author, André Theuriet, else I should not have known how to describe them.

The whole population of the countryside, men and women, are busy in the vineyards from early morn to dark, and the scene is most entertaining and informing. Our host was a master cooper, with a very considerable trade, a rather melancholy, absorbed man, with a bulbous nose "all limned by libidinousness" into a network of fine red veins. His trade, it may be urged, had too much and too intimate a relation with the seductive juice of the grape for him not to have a weakness for the "Soup of September," as it is sometimes called by the natives, in M. Theuriet's book, who relates of a wine grower: "To him came the care of many a customer's product, so quite naturally he had become a wine taster of considerable reputation. With the years his taste had refined, and in my mind's eye I can see him pour out a few drops of wine into a tall narrow glass and, sipping it with closed eyes, tell not only the date of its making, but the particular vineyard which produced it. Of his skill the following little story is told. Called to give his opinion of a certain wine, he said, after tasting it, 'This is good, but it has been in contact with iron and leather.' The grower was astonished, indignant, and denied that it had ever been out of the cask before, but lo, says the story, 'when the butt was empty, they found in the bottom a small piece of leather in which was an iron nail!' " And thus this man's fame spread over the country side.

In September the vine god grants his gifts of splendid ripe days and nights of radiance. From the slopes above the busy vineyards, one inhales the fragrance of the growing grapes, and scans the golden hillsides and the dim valleys with appreciative eyes. Over all the warm sun shines, gilding the roofs and spires, and bringing forth tender shadows among the trees. As the peasants say, poetically, for the peasants are poetic, although they do not know it, "The Virgin unwinds her distaff and spreads the golden threads over Alsace." Through the air, as clear as crystal, the workers can be heard calling to each other from hill to hill. Some of the badinage is coarse and the jests are often very unseemly, but you must remember that this very coarseness is a necessary part of the peasant's make up. He does not know that he is coarse or that his talk is unseemly. He thinks that he is witty, and nothing delights him more than that one should reprove him for some bit of repartee. This he will dwell upon for days thereafter, as proof of his brilliancy.

In the noonday sun the vineyards blaze in the transparent haze rising from the moist furrows of newly-plowed fields, where the laborers are toiling. These are called "vintagers," both men and women. They are, as a rule, hired by the week, and thus paid. They are from the country round, each squad, one is told, keeping to itself clannishly under an elected leader. The women are, as a rule, brawny and rarely pretty. They dress in short skirts or petticoats of gaily printed calico, and wear bodices and jackets of vivid colors. On their heads are short veils, or kerchiefs tied behind at the nape of the neck. Each woman carries an osier basket, in which she drops the fragrant grapes as she cuts them from the vine with a sharp bill-hook.

The married and unmarried are lodged in separate sheds, and furnished with coarse food by the proprietor. I was told that they earned thirty sous a day. For this meagre sum they toil from dawn to dark, but they are content and cheerful, although should you question one of them, at once, after the custom of the peasant under all circumstances, she will grumble and bewail her lot, and curse the rich proprietor who fattens upon the result of her toil.

In spite of this, the peasants look upon this work as

an agreeable change from their other toil. At early
dawn they are awakened by the call of the "Bellonier,"
he who carries the grapes to the wine press in a large tub
called a "Bellon." The half-asleep men and women
vintagers gather in the court with their baskets under
their arms, some of them yawning and rubbing their
eyes. One of the number with a good voice acts as
singer, and bellows out one of the vintage songs, of which
there are many. One had a chorus which ran something
as follows:

> "Aller au vendage
>   Pour gagner dix sous
> Coucher sur la paille
>   Ramasser des poux,
> Chante et danse
>   Toute comme un fou."

In the early morning hours, ere the sun has gotten its
full power, the best work is done, and the peasants perform their tasks with astonishing skill and energy. They
form in long lines, proceeding rapidly, stripping each
vine of its bunches, which they drop in their baskets.
These filled, they are emptied into large hampers, which
are held up by poles stuck in the ground. When the
hamper is filled the carrier who attends it lifts it to his
back and trots down the hillside to the "Bellon," which
is ready to receive it to transport it to the great wagons
standing under the shade of the trees. At one side are
tethered the large, heavy bodied, hairy-legged horses, and

hanging from the branches of the trees are the harnesses, all brass-mounted. The large collars of leather-covered wood are decorated with tassels and heavy cushions and stuffings of bright scarlet and pale blue wool. The scene is one of considerable picturesqueness. Imagine the feeding horses in the shadows, switching their tails at the flies; a laughing group of gaily-clad peasant girls coquetting with some of the young gallants. Where the sunbeams fall is a tall peasant, bareheaded, brown skinned, his loose blouse of brown linen open at the neck, showing the splendid development of muscles, pouring a stream of golden yellow grapes out of his basket into the wagon. Down through the thick, heavy foliage shines the sun in dusty beams of golden light upon his ruddy face, neck and bare arms. All about is ceaseless activity and animation, and over all is the strong, sweet odor of rich ripe grapes.

At the end of the day, when in the valleys the pale white mists form above the beds of the small streams, and the upper slopes swim in a hazy, warm glow from the final gleam of the departed sun, the word is given, and the "Bellonier," all bedecked with a green branch and surrounded by young girls, arm in arm, and followed by the hamper carriers and the cutters, descend the slope to the wagons, which are already in motion. Then homeward along the dim shady roads they take their way, singing the sweet, tender songs so dear to the peasants of the lost province. Can I make you see the picture as I see it?

Approaching the "Pressoir," where the grapes are pressed, they give loud calls, at which the great double doors are swung wide open, and the inside of the building, its roof supported by huge oaken beams, and fitted with immense round tubs, is plainly seen, and there, at the far end, around which strange figures appear mis-shapen in the flickering ruddy light of the large lanterns, is the brobdingnagian structure of the wine press, its beams all shining and dripping with the "must." Into its capacious maw is dumped the fragrant contents of the "Bellons." Round and round goes the great dripping beam, drawn by two huge hollow-backed horses in gaily-decked collars.—Round and round—to the sound of the women's roundelays, one of which, and a very popular one, goes something as follows:

> "The day is gone, and now its sweets
> Shall come. To thee, dear heart,
> To thee, dear heart.
> Sweet voice of thine; sweet lips and starry eyes;
> Come, let us clasp, and never, never part, dear heart,
> And never, never part."

and then the chorus:

> "From thee, dear heart,
> I'll never, never part."

It lingers in one's memory with something of painful insistence. The fragrant odor of new sweet wine exhales from the press. The whole place is saturated with it. Every cellar is filled with huge fat round-bellied casks, every gutter runs with the lees of wine. At night these small villages are filled with noisy laughter, and rather rough gaiety for these people who work so hard during the day must have their pleasures before midnight, when the local gendarme solemnly bids the cafés to close, and the workers to take themselves off to their straw heaps for the night. But until this hour yellow lights gleam and flicker in the windows of the houses, while from press to press are lines of large swinging oil lanterns hung overhead, lighting up the narrow lanes, with strange staggering, shifting, drunken shadows as the lanterns swing in the night air, and the long lines of heavily laden wagons come in from the distant vineyards.

The scene at suppertime in one of the large kitchens is an animated one. In the center is a long oaken table, lighted by kerosene oil lamps hanging from the whitewashed beams overhead. This table can seat as many as thirty at one time. The supper is of vegetable soup, very greasy, but savory and good, and there is plenty of dark bread and potatoes. The meat is generally salt pork, of which the peasant is inordinately fond. Sometimes a coarse, poor cheese is included, but not often. Of sweets there are none, but there is, of course, plenty of thin, watery wine provided, usually the second or third squeezing of the grape. The peasants feed noisily, and do full justice to the provender.

Supper over, they have just one desire—to dance. In each community is one large barn floor set apart for this purpose, and here both sexes caper and waltz or polka, until they well nigh drop with fatigue. Often, 'tis said, these affairs degenerate into orgies and quarrels, accompanied with the inevitable results. But it is very amusing to slip into a shadowed corner and from there watch one of these dances. At one side, upon a large upturned wine cask, is perched the "Jouer." It may be he is a fiddler, or perchance a piper from the town of Ferrette. At any rate there he sits, and beside him astride of a chair or stool is the dance master, calling out in loud tones the figures of the peasant dance. "Keep time, keep time, you," he calls to some unusually clumsy swain. "Where are your feet, Henri? You look like a duck in a hen yard." And then he will roar with laughter, clapping his hands to the rhythm of the dance. The fiddle squeaks or the pipe drones, the dust from the barn floor rises in clouds, and descends upon the bare heads and flushed faces of the young men and women. There is much good-natured jostling, and the noise of the heavy iron-shod clogs of the dancers is well nigh deafening; but it is all very dear to the peasants, and harmless enough, though at times there is considerable horseplay.

And so the days and nights of the vintage pass each

year until the last bunch is picked and pressed, and the rainy, dark days of early November bring the season to an end. Then the peasants scatter to their different villages for the winter, and the storks and cranes begin to fly in long lines toward the south, or wherever it is they nest in the dark wintry days.

In the narrow street under our windows one day was an excited group, composed of the proprietor of the Hotel, hatless, red-faced; a baker's boy in a long blue blouse and laden with two hampers of crisp brown loaves of bread; a girl carrying a solemn, wide-eyed baby, and a fat little man with a large saw, all gathered about the old carriage in which we had arrived a few days before. On the seat was the driver, recognizable by the faded blue coat with brass buttons—one could see no more of him than his knees and feet because of the carriage top. We speculated disinterestedly upon his presence there, because he had been well paid for his appreciated services and dismissed, as far as we were concerned.

But when we went down to the salon for coffee and rolls, we were at once summoned by the landlord, who gravely informed us that the driver had come for us, insisting that we were to depart at once upon our journey. In vain was it explained that we had no such purpose in view; that he had been paid and dismissed. The proprietor was plainly offended about something or other, and waved us forth to the doorway.

The old carriage was now surrounded by people who had gathered to know of the happening, whatever it might be, for the peasant loves a dispute of whatever nature, and apparently has unlimited leisure in which to enjoy it, more especially where a foreigner is involved. They gave way for me politely, and listened eagerly and breathlessly to my questions and the answers of the driver, who very plainly had, even at that early hour, a much heavier cargo of drink than he could well manage. In brief, he insisted that he felt it his duty, his simple duty—understand?—to Monsieur and the gracious Madame to look out for their welfare—to see that their journey was comfortable and safe—trust him for that; that they should not stop longer in Colmar where—yes, he would say it, and say it truthfully, too, in spite of any landlord, no matter who he might be—he would say it even to M. le Mayor himself, as an old soldier, who had served loyally his country and had his papers to show it, too. If this was not believed, all they had to do was to accompany him to his home and there, over the stove, hanging upon the wall, were those very papers framed in a good gilt frame to prove it. "Was not that enough? Eh, bien! Then why should not his word be taken? Had he not a good horse, too? Was he not well shod? Had he not paid for the shoeing that very week before he had the honor of conducting Monsieur and the gracious Madame on their safe journey? Then why had the landlord insulted him and attempted to keep him from guarding the interests of the distinguished strangers who had confided themselves to his protection? Would he depart without them? Would he leave them to their fate in Colmar? Not so! That never should be said against him—never!" and he beat his breast with his left hand while he waved and snapped his whip with his right.

"M'sieur has heard," said the landlord; "is it his wish that this man should remain?" I explained the circumstances of my agreement with the driver, and then turned to close the matter with him, while the loiterers listened eagerly, wagging their heads at each other, and grinning appreciatively. My words seemed to convey no meaning whatever to the driver, who was now gesticulating and nodding to the bystanders. Endeavoring to catch his eye, I saw that he was too far gone for any comprehension. Suddenly he burst into song—roaring out:

> "O! donnez moi jeunesse,
>   mon blonde—
> O! donnez moi jeunesse!—

the final words dwindling away in a hoarse, broken whisper, accompanied by copious tears and a despairing wave of the hand holding the whip, at which the fat horse awoke and started off so suddenly that the singer rolled out of his seat and would have fallen to the pavement had not a bystander caught him, while others stopped the horse.

Left reeling there on the pavement, the driver promptly sat down in the gutter, propped against a post, and went to sleep. The proprietor sent for the gendarme who, after hearing the history, entered our names in his book, saluted us, had him bundled into the old carriage, the bystanders took themselves off, and away went the old soldier, the fat horse and the lumbering old carriage, out of our ken. Thereafter we thought best to journey by train.

"Praise of the vintage," said the scholarly wine grower to whom I had been introduced and with whom I sat in the lovely old garden behind the mossy wall that surrounded his château on the river road, "should be uttered in the musical rhythm of poetry, which alone can convey the expression, like unto the most generous liquor pressed from the fragrant crushed grape.

"How else," he continued, "can one express the whispering of the fermenting; the liquid murmur of the bubbling 'must,' the song of the laboring great wine press as the oaken-bound beam swings around its circle in the cobwebby gloom, and the all pervading bouquet of the new running wine!" And then he went on in infinite detail of the art of wine making, telling how the sugary juice undergoes fermentation; how and why the grapes are crushed in wooden tubs at a certain temperature; how the skins and solid matter are removed by setting free the carbonic acid, forming on the surface of the

154

liquid what is called the "chapeau" of the vintage; that the juice extracted is still very sweet and is called "must"; and that put in strong casks it undergoes a second and slow fermentation, at which it arrives at the period of preservation and is fit for consuming. Thereafter he showed me the mysterious and most picturesque spectacle in one of the large "pressoirs" which he owned and operated.

Sometimes this scene may be enjoyed at night, and this is how I saw it, sitting with him in a corner of the large cellar, beneath the great rafters and oaken beams of his "pressoir," lighted by pendent oil lanterns, the ruddy glare from which illuminated fitfully the phantom-like figures of half naked men passing to and fro, or treading the masses of grape in the oaken tubs. A most singular low sort of buzzing or humming sound accompanies the fermentation, and in one's nostrils is a warm, most delicious, and semi-intoxicating odor exhaled from the crushing. Into large, burnished, ruddy, golden copper tubs spurts and drips the wondrous dark purple wine, flowing from the bed of the immense press in liquid, tinkling song. In the dim light of the lantern the naked bodies of the pressers gleam as they strain at the capstan beam which controls the screw of the press, while the huge machine groans complainingly, and forth beneath pours the new sweet wine. Men called porters empty the copper pans of the "must" into strangely-shaped vessels of wood named "tandelins," and laboriously carry them below to the cobwebby cellars far beneath. Hereabouts these cellars honeycomb the hills, which they penetrate for long distances, arranged in tiers or stories like catacombs, and the scene presents to the imagination something like an ancient religious rite. From them come strange booming sounds and echoes as the dimly-seen figures of the workmen come and go about their tasks.

The wine grower explained with great detail the importance of the soil and the climate in the production, alleging that the smallest change in the fertilization of the soil is sufficient to alter and even suppress the bouquet so necessary, rendering the product flat and useless. He explained the ancient law promulgated by the great Dukes of Lorraine, forbidding the use of manure in the Duchy under the most severe penalty, it having been proven that any attempt to enrich the sandy, stony hillsides, while increasing the size and quantity of the grapes, entirely destroyed the strange variety, and the unique and volatile bouquet. Here, then, in these vast catacombs hollowed in the "tufa" are miles of great casks of still and sparkling wines, laden with the odors of violets and honey, awaiting the days of their emancipation.

"Here, then, Monsieur," said he enthusiastically, raising his glass to the light of the overhead lantern, "French hearts are beating in patriotism and loyalty to the

Mother Country, from which, through no fault of ours, we are separated by the odious rule of the invader. Hail to the day of our release. Hail to the wines of Alsace-Lorraine. If our lips are silent over these evil days, our eyes bespeak our unwavering loyalty to France, our hearts understand.

"In the days when the English Queen Mary Stuart came to the castle of the great Dukes of Bar on the Ornain, was it not our wine of Alsace that delighted her, and inspired the Poet Ronsard at the banquet to recite in her honor these lines:

> "All things I do embrace
> And all things nourish:
> All things my virtue wakes to flourish:
> Bind I all things, my hands hold everything.
> Since this is true,—o'er all things rests my power,
> I bade expand this fragrant perfect flower,
> To rule the whole world over; this youthful King."

He related also tales of the early days, when at the banquets of the ecclesiastics for the visiting Cardinals of Trent at the time of the Council, the dignitaries proclaimed unanimously that the wines of Alsace were the noblest and most fragrant of all. And they drank to the glory of France.

"And what did you do all the evening?" asked Lady Anne when I returned to her at the château, where we were the guests of the erudite and scholarly wine grower and his lady. I related what had happened, with all the detail and embroidery at my command, and with considerable enthusiasm, too, I fancy. Lady Anne heard me with somewhat of a bored air, and remarked:

"How stupid; and is that all? I cannot abide those old gloomy, spidery cellars; and as for the wine, we had some here in the salon, and passed a delightful evening, for Madame got out all of her old embroidered linen, and taught me the most wonderful and exquisite stitch. I never saw such linen! Dozens and dozens of pieces. . . ."

Fête Days and Customs

Fête Days and Customs

THE feast days are perhaps best studied in the remote villages, because in the course of the peasant's hard life he has but few days of relaxation, and save for a wedding or a funeral rarely breaks away from his toil. So the Patron Saints' day is a real occasion for him to look forward to. In certain communities where the church still regulates the people's manners, it is the only day upon which dancing is permitted. Each department of France apparently has a different name for this fête. In upper Alsace it is known as the "Kilbe"; in the lower as "Mestig"—or sometimes Kirb; in the north it is "Ducasse"; "Rapport" in the east; "Vogue" in Dauphiny; "Assemblée" in Touraine; "Ballade" in Poitue; "Frairie" in Saintange and Angoumois, and the "Pardon" in Brittany.

In Alsace, however, the characteristics are quite different from those obtaining elsewhere. Instead of having the dances in various drinking resorts, the young people of the remote villages elect one of their number best fitted for the position, as organizer. He is thus the "Garçon d'honneur" of the fête. As distinctive sign of his position, he wears a cloak heavily embroidered in gold

161

lace.   To him falls the task of designing the festivities
and selecting the field where the dancing platform is
erected.   This is generally as near as possible to the local
inn or auberge.

In the remote towns on the day of the fête, a cortège
preceded by the local band of musicians, clad in their
archaic costumes, and bearing at the head the banner of
the association, all decked with flowers and ribbons, upon
which are fastened the various medals and prizes which
it has won, marches proudly to the house of the Mayor,
who receives the marchers in his official sash of honor and
proclaims the fête open.

The organizer then presents a bouquet with one hand,
and a bottle of wine with the other, to M. the Mayor.
Then, turning, he offers his little finger to the prettiest
girl, generally selected beforehand, and leading her at
the head of the procession, formed of both sexes, to the
dancing platform, opens the festivities.   In some localities a ribbon-decked lamb, led by the prettiest girl, pre-
cedes the cortège, and this poor little lambkin is then
killed somewhere out of sight, and dressed for the great
banquet to take place the following day.

This procession stops before the door of each of the
local magistrates or authorities, the "garçon d'honneur"
offering to each a portion of the great spice cake, which is
all covered with icing and colored ribbons; receives from
each a gift in return, (generally a small sum of money to

defray expenses), and the fête proceeds. (In certain of the villages, a masked figure, grotesquely costumed, is led in chains, by companions who take up a collection from the peasants as he passes along the streets. One we saw led to the village fountain, and there pitched neck and heels into the basin amid the wildest shrieks and cries from the crowd, who seemed infuriated at the sight. But when the creature was drawn out, and his soaked rags were stripped from him, he was given the money which had been collected, and promptly disappeared from sight.) This evidently is a very old custom, the origin of which is lost, for no one could satisfactorily explain to us what it was all about. The willing subject of this strange attack, I afterwards discovered, was a respectable young farmer who lived in the neighborhood. ·

The festivities continued throughout the day in a banquet in the "auberge," and a bonfire at night, around which the peasants danced hand in hand, after which they departed to their different homes. It was most amusing to watch the preparations for this particular celebration. The inn at which we stopped was the center of activities. In all the houses about the little square the housekeepers were busy in the kitchens, with arms bare to elbow, faces dusted with flour, kneading and pulling dough and forming all kinds of dainties. Over all was a most appetizing odor of baking pastry from blazing ovens. The night before arrived the jugglers and tumblers, and the huge vans of the itinerant merchants, who at once began to set up their stalls and booths in the spaces allotted to them by the watchful gendarme. At dawn the church bell rang loudly, calling the people to early mass. The young men soon appeared in the square, all freshly shaven, clad in all the unwonted finery of white linen shirt and stiff blouse. Behind the drawn curtains the young girls are arranging themselves before the mirrors in all their best, silk fichus and stiff standing-out headdresses of heavy black Alsatian silk called "noeuds." Very proudly they stand when they come forth, all in their wide stiff skirts, and heavy creaking shoes.

All go to the church on this day of high mass. It is crowded with the people, who are most devout, and the late ones who are unable to enter congregate on the steps. The service seems very long to the younger ones, who plainly are nervous and excited, and when at last the final prayer is said by the priest, they hasten away to "The Place" or square, where the musicians are already gathered, tuning up their shining brass instruments. Here also are the corps of "Pompiers," as the firemen are called, clad in quaint metal breastplates, and huge helmets with long horse hair plumes. The rest of the costume is most ludicrously ordinary, dwindling away from the splendor of the plumed helmet and shining breastplate, to patched corduroy trousers and hobnailed shoes.

But of these discrepancies they seem quite unconscious.

Early in the day the booths have been erected, each in the place allotted to the merchant. They contain everything calculated to tempt the peasant to spend his or her hard-earned coin. The young girls, with shining eyes, surround the pitiful display of caps and ribbons, cheap lace and gaudy skirts, eager to possess such treasures fresh from the great city. At one side is a fortune-teller, before whose tent a small darky, clad in oriental turban, parades ostentatiously, carrying a large green cockatoo on his outstretched wrist. At the other is a long scarlet wagon with a skylight, before which a hoarse-voiced Hebraic-looking man, wearing flashy jewelry, calls upon the peasants to "step up, pay up, and see the only living mermaid in captivity," which turns out to be a trained seal, and which certainly does its tricks with great intelligence and evident enjoyment. There is also an itinerant photographer, who for only one mark gives not only two likenesses "guaranteed," but a "gold" frame for one of them.

Loud beating of a large bass drum draws a crowd about a highly-varnished carriage, drawn by four large black horses with long manes and tails most beautifully groomed, and with oiled hoofs. The occupant, standing up on the seat, is calling for "amateurs" who wish to have their teeth drawn, "with no charge for the first one," whatever he means by that. Crowds of excited children dart hither among the people, eager to see it all at once. Older ones walk about cautiously clinking their coins together, trying to decide upon a purchase. Over all is the smell of hot fat from the waffle booth, where, over a hot coal fire, a fat, bare-armed woman is cooking the sweet dainties so beloved by the peasantry all over Europe. The inn and the small shops are full to overflowing with eating and drinking men and women. There is the raucous sound of a barrel organ, accompanied by loud singing, and from the open doors of the houses come servants carrying bottles and jugs to and fro. Amid shouts of laughter one hears glasses jingle and heavy hands pounding on the tables. The costumes are brilliant in color and unusual.

The women, young and old, wear the huge bow of black ribbon ("noeud Alsatian") on their heads. Occasionally, however, in some of the groups the ribbons will be of red or plaid, or even ornamented with large, bright flowers. The skirts are varied in color, some of striped purple, others in quaint squares or checks. The waists or bodices are most lavishly embroidered in bright colors, and the collars are often of very fine and valuable lace. The size of the headdress varies with the locality. For instance, those of Oberseebach and Hoffen are quite small and generally of dark red silk. The cut of the skirt is also different. It would take a whole chapter to describe in detail the variety of costumes of the provinces.

FÊTE DAYS AND CUSTOMS

I am informed that there are at least fifty different styles in existence, but that since the invasion of the provinces the peasants have refrained from wearing many of them, out of contempt for the Germans. The ancient costumes are almost extinct in the lower Rhine region from Sainte Odile to the Palatinate frontier. In the towns of the Upper Rhine they are now rarely seen save at Metzeral, and in the Fecht valley, at Sundernach near Munster. In the Vosges, and the Sundgau, the more conservative of the peasantry still wear the distinctive "noeuds," but to see them as they were formerly worn one must seek them on fête days or Sundays. Usually the costumes differ but little from those worn elsewhere in France.

One of the greatest fête days is that of Belfort, sometimes called and spelled "Befort," a town and fortress of the first class on the river Savoreuse, a place of the greatest military importance commanding the famous passage between the Vosges and the Jura, called the gap of Belfort. The town is an ancient one, having been founded in the eleventh century, although but little evidence of this antiquity is now to be seen. The house of Burgundy acquired it in marriage in the fourteenth century, and it then passed on successively to those of Ferrette and Austria. It was taken by the Swedes in 1632, and by the French in 1636 and 1648. In 1814 it successfully resisted the Allies, and also the siege by the

ALSACE-LORRAINE

Germans in 1870–71, which lasted from November, 1870, to February, 1871, and capitulated with the honors of war only upon conclusion of an armistice and under orders from the French government. The old town is on the left bank of the river and commanded by a most imposing looking citadel upon the lofty summit of a rock, said to be more than 200 feet high. Before it is the colossal statue of the Lion of Belfort, the work of Bartholdi. Beyond the Porte de Brisach is a hollow, where there is an immense entrenchment, in which, it is said, twenty thousand men can be encamped. Through it passes the high road to Strassburg. Beyond this is the famous Fort de la Miotte, with its tower, which is considered the very Palladium of Belfort, a sacred heritage. This tower, it is said, was almost entirely destroyed during the Franco-Prussian war, but has since been reconstructed. Here each year come conscripts and their families by the thousands, who venerate the sacred object, which is a small stone from the original tower set in the wall.

Among these simple country people, strangely enough, there seems to be no fear of death. We found that one thought alone horrifies and gives them anxiety; that is the fear of Hell, and the terror of encountering the ghosts of those who die unrepentant and without having confessed to the priest. In the remote villages of the Vosges, as soon as a peasant is judged to be on his or her deathbed, he or she is at once arranged for the final moment, even though the end is a day or so distant. The neighbors are notified, and the house is open to all, whether day or night. Thither the neighbors come to pay their respects and condole with the family. All visit the bed where the poor creature lingers, already regarded as having gone beyond the pale. A basin displayed upon a white towel contains holy water, and in this is a green branch, which is used by all to sprinkle the bed on which the sick peasant is lying on his back, his hands already crossed upon his breast. In and out of the room passes the procession of people, who are moved often as much by curiosity as interest. It is most pathetic, not to say uncanny. After the end comes, the deceased is attended by a watch formed of the relatives and certain aged women, who make a sort of profession of waiting with the corpse.

Our driver informed us that they take turns in watching during the night, "driving away evil spirits, drinking much hot wine and spices in the intervals of exorcism, and that they compose poems in eulogy of the dead." We imagined these services to be somewhat like the Irish wakes, or the Corsican "Voceri." The driver repeated some of the exclamations, which were: "Ah, the poor man, why did he die?—and so early too, and he not yet forty! Ah, that I should have to cry at his funeral—Sainted Marie!"—and so on.

He told us that, as a usual thing, the coffined body is

borne to the church on a bier; but if that of a young girl, her companions always carry her body, and they are always veiled and clad in pure white, and that a lighted taper is carried before the procession by her nearest and dearest friend. In the case of a youth or a man, the friends always walk on foot in procession, all wearing bands of crêpe on their arms and hats. The men and women walk separately. After the burial, all the friends and neighbors are invited to the bereaved home for a feast, known as the "obit," for the peasants are great eaters and drinkers. This feast begins in great solemnity, but as it progresses and the bottles are emptied, the talk grows louder and louder, until the oldest friend of the deceased rises and eulogises him, and then all join in intoning a sort of a "de profundis." Then after a collection is taken up for the poor, the ceremony is over.

The peasants regard unfailingly all anniversaries, and do not fail to see that mass is said by the priest for the repose of the soul of the departed. All Saints' day is, however, particularly the day upon which the villagers visit the cemetery to pay homage to their dead, and the scene of the green mounds surrounded by kneeling women and men in the shadow of the creamy white walls of the village church is very moving. The peasants bring green branches, which are blessed on Palm Sunday, and decorate the graves. These are, in some places, called "Pagnottes," and remain through the year into the winter, until the white mantle of snow has covered all from sight.

One of the curious observances is the Choral Fête du Dimanche, held in the neighborhood of Strassburg, and on the Palatinat frontier, when bands of young girls congregate in the localities in large numbers in the evening after vespers, and, hand in hand, parade the streets of the villages, singing the quaint and often very musical folk songs of ancient Alsace. Nothing more exquisite can be imagined than the sweet voices of these young girls sounding among the thick trees. The songs are adorable in their sentiment. However, I am told that since the enforcement of the hated "Wacht am Rhein" at all concerts and gatherings, the custom has gradually ceased.

Another strange custom is that called the "Assemblée," where the proprietors and farmers meet to hire young maids, shepherds and laborers to work on the farms. Sometimes these occasions are called "louées," and take place during the day in the public square, or even out in the open fields outside of the towns. The young girls or fellows who wish work wear branches of leaves at their waists, or in their hats. A green branch thus announces, "Hire *me*, please, I am stout, able and strong, and I pledge myself and my labor faithfully to you for one year at the price of fifty francs, my clothes, and good food to eat."

ALSACE-LORRAINE

The farmers in search of labor stop at the inn, which is decorated with branches of pine or juniper, and always the bargain is concluded over a bottle of wine. The agreement signed on both sides—it is always in writing and minutely worded—the retainer of five francs paid, back go the boys and girls to the dancing. The hurdy-gurdy squeals and groans and snuffles, the archaic bag-pipe drones, and over all is heard the voice of the dance leader calling out hoarsely the figures of the "quadrille." How the skirts fly about as the strong-armed peasant boys swing their flushed-faced partners! How anxious they all are for a day or so of pleasure before they begin their year of hard, grinding toil—early morn to dark, and then, after a bowl of soup and a thick crust with half a bottle of thin wine, they tumble into their straw for the few hours' rest allowed them. What wonder that they drink to excess on this their day of freedom, in forgetfulness of all that lies before them!

This sort of gathering may be studied at Bouxwiller, a most charming and delightful little town in the neighborhood of Saverne. It was at this place that the Alsatian painter, Maréchal, made many of the studies for his pictures. In Alsace, we are told, when two young people have been attracted to each other and exchanged vows, they present themselves before their parents dutifully and ask their authority. As a rule this authority is rarely withheld, and the couple are henceforth permitted to go and come as they will, to attend fêtes at distant towns together, and even to stop at inns for days at a time without any sort of restraint or scandal. Their faith is plighted, and that is enough. This is similar to the Dutch custom. A few days before the wedding they appear before the town notary and sign the civil wedding contract.

Sometimes, in certain localities, the young girl is then expected to disappear coyly and hide herself away in some corner of the house. All the parties then join gaily in the search for her, and it may be said that, as a rule, she is not hard to find. Then she is forcibly carried before the notary, and by certain promises and the payment of a silver present by the prospective groom, she finally, amid shrieks of laughter and somewhat free jokes, consents to add her signature to the contract, which is then duly stamped by the notary and delivered into the hands of the young girl, or her parents or guardian, as the case may be. A great dinner is then given by the parents, sometimes in the "Salle des Noces" at the inn, and there are merry or tearful speeches by those who feel so moved, and every one eats and drinks immoderately to the health of the young couple, who sit at the head of the long table, holding hands and beaming upon each other and all the world besides. At the end of the dinner, which lasts for hours, shots are heard outside, and immediately, amid great shouts and applause, two or three young fellows in uniform, conscripts of the year, burst in upon them. One of these presents a huge bouquet of flowers to the fiancée, with a humorous verse suited to the occasion. The others then come forward and recite in unison a poem of more or less freedom, calling down blessings upon the pair. These compliments concluded, the young pair present the three well-wishers with a sum of money in silver, called the "trumbolle," which later on is spent at the inn in celebration.

Elsewhere upon the day of marriage the groom and his groomsmen, all dressed in their best, parade the streets in a carriage, all decked with flowers and ribbons, delivering the invitations to the wedding. A pistol shot fired outside the house announces their arrival. The groom then invites the inmates, with a well-turned compliment, takes a glass of wine, and passes on to the next house. As the invitations are many in a wedding of this sort, it is perhaps needless to comment upon the condition of the groom and his cohort of honor before they finish their task. The day before the ceremony the furniture and belongings of the couple are transported with great ceremony in one or two large wagons to their future home. The wagons are drawn by as many horses as the groom can afford, and both wagon and horses are most lavishly decorated with ribbons and wreaths of flowers. The first wagon is driven by the groom himself, and contains the nuptial couch, all set up and dressed with fine linen and embroidery. The next contains the chairs, wardrobe and pots and pans of iron and bright new copper. In the last wagon is the cradle, all hung with ribbons and wreaths, and two or three young girls all in the glory of the costume of the village. Should the procession have to pass through any neighboring village street, the cortège is held up by the boys and girls, and the groom is forced to pay a small ransom for permission to proceed.

On the wedding day, the invited guests march to the house, carrying personally the wedding gifts. A loud peal from the church bell announces the presence at the church of the groom and his family. At the second stroke of the bell the best man, accompanied by the maid of honor, goes to the presbytery and presents to the priest or clergyman the so-called "Soupe Nuptial," contained in a small tureen, together with a trencher of roast meat. The best man also offers in turn a bottle of old wine, garlanded with flowers, and a slice of bread.

The ceremony then commences. When the happy pair emerge from the bride's house they are greeted by shots from fowling pieces, and loud shouts of welcome from the crowd awaiting them. The procession then forms, at the head walks the groom, his hat ornamented with a sprig of "romarin," arm in arm with the maid of honor. Following these comes the bride, on the arm of the best man. Then follow the parents, relatives and friends, in their order.

After the ceremony the pair are stopped by the choir, when the wedding is Catholic, and by the orphans of the town, when Protestant, and these, holding a long ribbon or garland, forbid passage until the customary sum of money is paid. Returning to the home of the parents for the wedding banquet, the bride and groom and the invited guests take part in certain "Pantagruelistic" festivities, varying more or less, according to locality, but sometimes of a character which cannot well be described in print. The following day the guests are invited to a dance and supper, which is prolonged far into the night. On the third and last day of the celebration, the best man and his assistants proceed to the home of the maid of honor, and secure the hoe and the "quenouille" (distaff) offered by the friends to the newly-married couple. A procession forms in great state, preceded by a couple of musicians playing cornets. Two young girls in costume carry the hoe and the "quenouille," and proceed to the new house of the bride and groom, to whom they offer them most solemnly. A collection is then taken up by a parish officer for the benefit of the poor; these are never forgotten, no matter what the occasion.

M. Henry Welschinger (member of the Institute) in his delightful account, "Moeurs et coutumes," speaks of one ceremony which, however, we did not see. "There is a very amusing wedding custom in the environs of Soultz-sous-Forêts. At a certain moment of the day the guests behold the great door of the farmhouse open, amid cries of delight and laughter. One hears an oft-repeated phrase shouted by the crowd of onlookers, 'D'r yle wangen Kompt' (dialect), as a cavalier, mounted on a horse, all clad in garlands and ribbons, appears, blowing a long brass trumpet. The horse is attached to a large cart wheel by means of a chain, and on the wheel are seated the grotesquely attired figures of a man and a woman, with huge false noses, and uttering loud cries of simulated terror as they are dragged along, clinging frantically to the revolving wheel's rim.[1] What is the signification of this strange ceremony? No one can explain exactly. It is certainly of great antiquity, perhaps it betokens the vicissitudes of married life, or typifies the character of the road before them. . . ."

The wedding feasts are always prolonged to the very last degree, for the peasants are great eaters and drinkers. The food provided is abundant, often costing far more than they can well afford, through pride, and resulting sometimes in the accumulation of debts, under which the parents labor for years. But they do not grudge the expense, even though it entails such suffering. Roast birds and stewed meats, with huge patties and all sorts of tarts

---

[1] Just how this was accomplished was not made clear by the author.

and pastry abound. At the groaning table in the always picturesque dining room, the happy-faced bride and groom are seated at the head of the gathering, with the relatives and honored guests, generally in the order of age. The younger folk, boys and girls, are placed together at one side, and are very noisy and full of quips and loud laughter over the usually very free conversation. It is customary for the notables, M. the Mayor if possible, to drink the health of the bride in a felicitous speech, and this is afterwards boasted about and discussed by the family long after the festivities have become dim memories in the neighborhood. After the Mayor has shaken hands with the couple, wished them long life and departed, comes the musical part of the festivity, in which the ushers and the young girl friends of the pair take turns in singing the well-known sentimental songs of the province, and then, amid cheers and applause, the door opens and in come the old women who have perchance cooked and labored over the banquet. These arrange themselves about the bride and groom and solemnly chant the "Bride's Song," usually of a most lugubrious character—grave and melancholy, suited, as they think, to the life of the peasant, filled with allusions to toil, trouble, and bereavement. After all the noise and laughter, it lends a tragic note to the celebration, and there are tears, and sad shakes of gray heads over the well-known words of such meaning to those who have

travelled the worn road of life. The singers present a
bouquet to the bride, singing something like this:

> Pray take these flowers from me, Madame,
> For soon you'll plainly see, Madame,
> These happy hours—
> These fragrant flowers
> Shall turn to dust—
> As all things must—
> Soon you shall plainly see, Madame!—Soon you shall
> plainly see!

Then all at once the musicians make a loud noise with
their instruments, which quite drowns the lugubrious
song, and the old women are hustled away, rewarded
with a couple of pieces of silver each for their trouble,
and all leave the disordered table for the dance in the
barn, or on the grass in the meadow, if the weather is
fine. During the dance the bride and groom steal away
to some neighboring house, in which they are to stop for
the night, the secret of which they think has been jealously guarded, but all in vain, for their flight is soon remarked and the search begins. They are soon discovered
and the sound of a gun-shot draws the crowd to their
retreat, where one of the ceremonies is the presentation
of a bowl of "white soup" by the best man and the maid
of honor to the couple in the chamber, while outside the
house the young people dance and sing until they are
wearied. One of the "Chansons of La Saintange," of

which the peasants are very fond, runs something like this:

> Your husband sure you'll find,
> Will rule you and control you!
> He'll not be always kind,
> And who will then console you?
> But always let him have his way,
> For certainly you must obey . . .
> Heh! la la, Heh! la la!

And thus rises the curtain upon the married life of the peasant.

Another very quaint ceremony is called the "Guller-tanz" (Rooster Dance), celebrated in the neighborhood of Ingwiller (Lower Alsace). It is described as taking place in the large barns, where there is ample floor space. There will be a tall pole, all garlanded with vines and flowers, and hung with flags, from among which the beloved tri-color is missing. To this pole is suspended the prize rooster of the community. All about the huge room in the barn, with its great dark, roughly-hewn oaken beams crossing overhead from wall to wall, are seated the young girls and their parents, and promenading up and down in pairs are the eligible young men from far and near, all dressed in their best holiday array. Thus the young people are able to meet and become acquainted properly under the watchful eyes of their parents or guardians. After half an hour of this promenading and introducing, the master of ceremonies gives the signal, and the young girls form a circle about the flower-decked pole and intone a joyous sort of Rabelaisian poem, in which some of the sentiments are rather free in language; too much so for quotation here. But it is quite a matter of course in these country districts of Alsace-Lorraine. This concluded, the girls choose their partners and the dance begins. Above where the rooster is hanging there is suspended horizontally a stick, wrapped in ribbons, upon which is fixed a large tallow candle. At each end of this stick is a cord; suspended from one is a bottle; from the other a leaden ball. When the signal is given to begin the dance, the first couple are handed a bouquet of flowers, which together they hold as high as they can reach, while dancing about the pole. When they tire, they pass the bouquet to the couple next behind, and so on up to the moment when the tallow candle burning down sets fire to the string and lets fall either the leaden ball or the bottle. The dancers who carry the bouquet at this moment win the prize rooster, but this would seem an expensive sort of prize, for he or she who gains it is required to serve it up roasted at the supper which follows the ceremony, and the young man is expected to furnish the wine to wash it down. But I am told the penalty is always paid with very good grace.

In Lorraine on one of the Sundays of "Carême," a singular custom is maintained by the peasants. For weeks before they gather and prepare great torches made of hay steeped in resin. When the day arrives, a parade takes place, headed by the local band of fiddlers and pipers, and followed by gaily decorated farm wagons, drawn by great draft horses, and filled with young men, girls, and laughing, shouting children. This celebration is called "Büre," in some localities; in others "Le feu des Brandons et des Burés," and also in the dialect "Bauernfartnacht." Children make the round of the village, knocking gaily at the doors and begging faggots and all sorts of fuel for the fire. This they pile in the wagons and carry to the place where the celebration is to be held, generally in the public square of the village. There the fuel is made into a great pile, and at a signal, after darkness has fallen, a match is put to it, and as the flames light up the scene, the peasants dance about it and sing their sometimes merry and often melancholy folk songs. In the valley when the "burés" are set on fire, the young boys and girls gather with lists of the names of their companions. Against each name of a young fellow the master of ceremonies places the name of a young girl, and these are then considered affianced for the evening. When the "brandon" or "buré" is set on fire, two young fellows, elected previously, are placed in the window of one of the houses overlooking the scene. By the aid of a lantern the list is read as follows:

The reader cries out loudly: "I specify, I specify." The waiting crowd below cry out gleefully:

"Whom do you specify?"

"Alphonse Dargon and Marie Dieudonné."

"'Tis done, and well done!"

Then some one fires off a musket or fowling piece, and the spectators proceed with the game or ceremony until all the names have been read out to the end of the list.

Sometimes, so it is said, this arbitrary coupling of the names of the young people results in weddings. The young girls who are pleased with their oddly-named partners, invite these "fiancés" to their homes, with the consent of the parents, and it is then customary for the young couple to seat themselves side by side for the fête day supper. After this, should the families be pleased, they exchange visits very formally, with a view to the business of marriage between the young people.

These customs vary according to locality; in some of the towns in the Vosges on this particular Sunday in "Carême," the parading couples so curiously brought together, are called "Valentins" and "Valentines," and these are required to dance together about the great bonfire, to the accompaniment of a fusilade of gunshots, and the joyous cries and laughter of the crowd. After which they exchange gifts, and visit each other's parents, until the engagement is an accomplished fact.

It is said that quite often this coupling of names is prearranged by the parents, and that, at any rate, a couple so named are not expected to object, for any reason, or to refuse to dance together. This would be considered in very bad taste, to say the least. Each locality has its peculiar celebrations, varying most interestingly, embodying sometimes charming details, and at others astonishing ones, but all singularly free from that coarseness generally looked for in peasant gatherings.

Sainte Odile

Sainte Odile

ON the crest of the mount of Sainte Odile, near Obernai, is the great and celebrated convent standing like a crown above the dark trees. The "culte" of this illustrious saint, who is the "patron" of Alsace, embraces the memories of Charlemagne, Richard Cœur de Lion, Louis le Debonnaire, and not only Charles IV, but many other Emperors and Kings, not to mention the countless number of other great personages down to the present day, and still attracts multitudes of pilgrims and visitors, who contribute to the renown of the Convent, coming from the most distant towns as well as from Strassburg, Colmar and Schlestadt. Many of the painters of France, as well as those of Alsace, such as Jundt and Lix, have found subjects here for their pictures. Each year the representatives of upwards of twenty-four parishes walk in procession to the tomb of the saint on the mount. The place of pilgrimage is most picturesque, and whoever attends one of these pilgrimages is well re-paid by the view of the immense dark forests which surround the mount, through which the winding white roads seen here and there among the great trees are like silvery ribbons. The high towers of the church and the chapel of the saint against the sky, and below, the exquisite flowering gardens, all make a most unusual picture. Above the high wall is the ancient Hohenburg, the château of Adalric, who was Duke of Alsace, father of Sainte Odile. From this tower one may view the immense green and golden plains of cultivated fields; the lines of tall poplars; the vineyards, and the small dim villages of clustered peaceful-looking houses, with their rosy tiled roofs; the spires of the quaint whitewashed churches; and the distant silvery ribbon of the Rhine, where rises the mistily-seen towers of Strassburg's Notre Dame, or the snow-capped mountains of Switzerland.

At the side of the terrace, overhanging a precipice, is found the Chapel of the Angels, erected, it is said, in commemoration of a celestial apparition seen by Sainte Odile, in which she had a vision of the sufferings of her father in purgatory, from which her fervent prayers delivered him. On Sainte Valentine's day, each year, hundreds of young girls of the neighborhood make a pilgrimage to the convent, in which is a miraculous fountain, said to be a cure for all diseases of the eye. Others come to make nine turns of the tower, "which," the custode naïvely informed us, "assures their wedding within the year."

Near the Convent, upon a plateau, is the celebrated "mur païen," the remains of an ancient Celtic fortifica-

tion, said to be "more than two thousand years old."
This is one of the great monuments of Alsace. Its proportions are gigantic, encircling as it does the whole
mountain and enclosing in the neighborhood of "one
hundred hectares." (A hectare equals two acres, one
rod and thirty-five perches.) This great wall is believed
to have been constructed by the Celts to serve as a refuge
for the inhabitants of the region during the Gallo-Roman
epoch, and was enlarged by the Romans at various times
as defense against the Germanic invasions. Lucian
makes reference to it in "Pharsale" (Vol. I, pp. 354–
357). The wall is two or three yards high in some
places, and is formed of great cut stones and joined together by oaken pegs, which pegs have, of course, rotted
away, but the connecting holes are plainly to be seen.
It is said by authorities that this mode of fastening was
common to the Roman masons. At any rate, no trace of
mortar or cement is to be seen among the stones. Here
is shown the great stone called the "Minnelstein,"
through the "eye" of which, as in the case of the "Sorcerer's Eye," before mentioned, a remarkable panorama
of the valley is to be had. A little farther on is found an
immense rock, attached to the "enciente," standing more
than thirty feet high, called the "Wachtstein," used as a
post of observation during various wars, and dominating
the environing valley. .

In the Colmar region is celebrated yearly the pilgrim-

age of Notre-Dame des Trois Épis, which serves for the
Upper Rhine as the pilgrimage of Sainte-Odile does for
the Lower Rhine, with the difference, however, that
Sainte Odile is of the greater importance as the Patron
Saint of Alsace. This has certain unique characteristics
that distinguish it from all others. For instance the
most pious walk barefooted from the remote villages,
chaplet in hand, reciting their prayers in a loud voice.
The celebration takes place in the Commune of Amer-
schwirh, canton of Kaysersberg. According to tradi-
tion, a sacrilegious peasant at mass threw his portion of
the Holy Sacrament on the ground. Afterwards it was
found miraculously suspended upon "Trois Épis," where
the honey bees had enveloped it with wax. In celebration of this miracle, a pilgrimage was inaugurated by the
priests. The great beauty of the site of the church, set
amid a magnificent forest on the mountain draws people
from distant parts of the country each year. The Convent itself is not remarkable, although built in 1635.
The interior is quite filled with "Ex Votos," and a heavy
ornamentation. On the wall is shown a stone bearing a
bizarre mark, said to be the imprint of the Evil One,
placed there during a terrific storm that occurred while
the Chapel was being constructed.

Nearly two hundred years after the Franks drove the
Alamans back from Strassburg, that is to say, about the
year 660, and in the reign of Adalric (or Ethicon), duke

of Alsace, and his spouse Béreswinde, a babe was born to them, a girl, and to their grief she was blind. Adalric from despair turned to desperation, and in his passion and disappointment would have killed the child, had not the mother secretly confided it to the care of the faithful nurse who attended her. The child, secreted, was taken by night to a distant part of the forest, where it grew up in the family of a poor wood-cutter, and eventually was baptised by a holy man, and given the name of Odile. During the ceremony the girl miraculously recovered her sight, and word of this reaching the ears of the Bishop, she was sent for and brought to a distant monastery.

Meanwhile her father, Adalric, ever a man of violence, had killed his well beloved son in a fit of passion. And while doing penance in remorse, his wife, finding him thus softened in spirit, confessed to him that the girl who had recovered her sight so miraculously and whose name was on every lip throughout the dukedom, was none other than the daughter whom he had tried to kill. Adalric, overjoyed, sent for her, and bestowed upon her the Château of Hohenbourg, which she afterwards made into a monastery, and this is the convent which bears to-day the name of the blind girl Odile.

At the foot of the mountain she built another monastery, to which the name of Niedermunster was given. Here she planted three of the great trees for which the monastery is renowned. Sainte Odile died "at a great age, on the thirteenth of December, in the year 730." It is remarked that many of the young girls of the region bear the name of Odile, and this is so because Sainte Odile is the patron saint of all Alsace; the thirteenth of December is the day of her fête, and her tomb on the mountain of Sainte Odile, one of the highest peaks of the Vosges, is the most venerated among the Alsatians.

The Quaint Houses

The Quaint Houses

I CANNOT do better than quote the description of the houses given so admirably by M. Anselme Langel:

"The houses are usually in two stories; the first, a sort of 'rez de chaussée' above the cellar, contains a vestibule, from which mounts the stairs, the kitchen, and two chambers, one usually with two windows opening on the street, occupied by the master, and the other, much smaller, on the inner court. The interiors are immaculately clean, the floors scrubbed and covered with fine white sand. The ceilings, with beams exposed, are of boards painted brown and highly varnished. Often in the center of the room will be a wooden post heavily and lavishly carved, and sometimes picked out with rosettes of pale red or green paint, which upholds the center beam. The furniture of the principal room is that of an apartment used jointly as dining room and bedroom; one of its sides is formed by a partition in which are two large open-work carved doors, through which is had a view of the monumental beds, all hung with curtains and showing treasures of embroidered sheets and pillow cases. This is a country in which the mattresses and pillows assume immense proportions, rendering the ceremony of going to bed a sort of gymnastic performance, not always enjoyed by the stranger. Between the doors of this apartment, or alcove, as it should be called, stands the clock, considered one of the most important pieces of household furniture, upon which much money and care is expended. 'The beating heart of the household,' it is called. The high benches affixed to the walls are opposite to the great table, before which are arranged the highly-carved and painted chairs. In a corner is built a huge press, an indispensable part of every well-ordered household. This is generally a superb piece of cabinet work, and contains the trousseau of the mistress of the house. It is lavishly carved and decorated by gorgeous rosettes and flowers painted in red, yellow, blue, green and gold. A great stove of iron and porcelain occupies a considerable part of one side of the room, with large pipes and carriers connected with the beams overhead. Of a square form at base, it is rounded above like a column, and topped off by an urn or ornamental finial.[1] Above the stove is a rack or series of poles, upon which clothes may be hung to dry. Behind the stove is a sort of cabinet of shelves, upon which are various pots and pitchers used in the cuisine. On the wall usually there will be an ornamental

[1] My drawing shows such an interior and stove as M. Langel describes. Author.

mirror, and various small frames containing photographs, sacred pictures, or the diplomas belonging to the owners' military service.

"The kitchen opens opposite the main door and the small vestibule; it is generally quite roomy, and contains the bin and the oven in which the bread is baked. The oven protrudes outside the wall of the house and looks something like a large mushroom growth beneath the low eaves of the roof of the kitchen extension. Here each week, on Saturday, which is bake day, the week's supply of bread is baked. Opening on the kitchen is another room, where the young people may sleep, or maybe it is a sort of grain house, according to need. Beside the house are grouped the various dependencies, such as the stable, or carriage house, or what not.

"The Alsatian houses always bear, in some form or other, the date of construction and the name or initials of the proprietor. The most ordinary dates seen are those of 1790 to 1825. It is easy to see that following the Revolution, there arose in the soul of the peasant a 'sentiment of property,' and he proudly placed in his housefront, above the date, the name of his family or that of his wife. At Schleithal, for example, I have found the following on a gable: 'Anduni Armbrust i March den 1ar Republik' (Antoine Armbrust built me in the first year of the Republic). This is a rare example of revolutionary notation, for one finds generally that they follow the calendar, with the dates simply, such as 1792, or 1794.

"The habitations of the Lorraines differ radically from those of Alsace. In construction they recall the meridionals, with flat roofs of tile. The houses are low, and very well planned, divided curiously in their length into two parts; one in which they live, the other for what may be called 'exploitation.' The lodging part is generally composed of two chambers and a kitchen. There are rarely chambers on the second floor. This space is always reserved for a granary or storage place. The end of the kitchen is occupied by an enormous pyramidal open chimney, in which is suspended for curing, pork and hams or long links of the succulent sausage of Lorraine. From this room open two chambers with huge mountains of beds, elaborately trimmed with embroidered quilts and pillows themselves as big as feather beds. The domestics generally sleep either in the kitchen, or in the stable adjoining."

Except in the more remote villages of the provinces of Alsace-Lorraine, one rarely now comes upon the spinning wheel.

Up to the time of the Franco-Prussian war, however, I am told that they were quite commonly in use, and formed one of the principal occupations for women. Andrew Lang, writing of the idyl upon the distaff in the works of Theocritus, says:

THE QUAINT HOUSES

Distaff, blithely whirling distaff, azure-eyed Athene's gift,
To sex the arm and object of those whose lives is households' thrift,
Seek with me the gorgeous city raised by Neilus, where a plain
Roof or pale green rush o'erarches Aphrodite's hallowed fame,
Thither ask I Zeus to waft me, fain to see my old friend's face,
Nicias, o'er whose birth presided every passion-breathing Grace;
Fain to meet his answering welcome; and anon deposit thee
In his lady's hands, thou marvel of laborious ivory.
Many a manly robe ye'll fashion, and much floating maiden's gear,
Nay, should e'er the fleecy mothers twice within the self same year
Yield their wool in yonder pasture, Theugenis of the dainty feet
Would perform the double labor; Matrons' cares to her are sweet."

Lang notes that the idyl accompanied the present of a
distaff, which Theocritus brought home from Syracuse to
Theugenis, wife of his friend Nicias, the physician of
Miletus. On the margin of a translation by Longpierre
(Theocritus, Idyl XXVII, translated by S. C. Calverly)
Louis XVI wrote that this idyl is a model of honorable
gallantry.[1] Occasionally now one will be found in a
country home on the top of a quaint old wardrobe, made
of pear wood inlaid with ebony and ivory, with light,
most gracefully fashioned legs, its turned cap and high
bobbin and distaff tied with faded ribbons, suggesting a
whole life of laborious solitude and peaceful contemplation of passing events. The distaff may sometimes be
seen in use at the present day in the household in the
evening. And once we came upon a girl in the fields
spinning skeins with a spindle while tending her sheep,

[1] André Theuriet.

199

recalling the pictures of Bastien Le Page. This is the
simplest and most ancient form of spinning. She held
in one hand a stone, to which the bunch of hemp was fastened; and with the other she pulled and twisted the
tow, which she moistened with saliva, and thus transferred into thread, winding it around the spindle, to
which she gave a rotating motion.

The wheel is, of course, more complicated, the bobbin
taking the place of the distaff, while a pewter cup of
water fastened to the post serves to moisten the thread,
which is drawn, twisted and fixed on the bobbin, which
when filled is reeled off and made into skeins by means of
an instrument called the "Giroinde," now rarely met
with, as it has almost entirely vanished as a piece of furniture. It may be seen in Chardin's paintings, however.
It is a kind of reel, mounted on a pedestal, and has the
shape of a wheel each spoke of which, however, is a
branch terminating in a vertical pin. This wheel is
operated by the hand instead of the foot, and the thread
from the bobbin winds about the circular pins in such a
manner as to make the skein. I am told that in the winter the wheel is used in the long evenings when the young
girls gather at some arranged rendezvous in one of the
large farm house kitchens, lighted by candles and oil
lamps supplied by each comer. Young men come too,
bringing with them large bundles of faggots to burn in
the wide fireplace, and baskets of provender such as

cheese and sausages for the evening's feast. The host usually supplies plenty of the light wine of the neighboring vineyard, and loaves of bread. While the wheels are humming and tongues are going, all the news of the region is exchanged. The births, engagements and marriages, especially the latter, are discussed at length. All the love affairs of the region are twisted and woven and tangled into the skeins on the bobbins. These are occasions welcomed by the boys and girls, who thus come to flirt and coquet, the only chance they have, indeed. And here are told the best tales of ghost and adventure, for the store of these is inexhaustible.

Dreien-Eguisheim

Dreien-Eguisheim

JUST beyond Colmar, overlooking the small village of Eguisheim, which boasts extravagantly of it, is a recently restored palace (but the inhabitants call it a "Pfalz" in their quaint jargon) said to date back to the eighth century. This, by the way, was so scraped of stone and shiny with paint that I could not get interested in it. The unmistakable marks of German restoration were all over the place. Then again the custode, "appointed from Berlin," he informed me grandiosely, was otherwise so offensive that I turned my back upon him. A mile from the village stand the ruins of the great three towered castle of Hohen-Eguisheim, generally called the Dreien-Eguisheim or Exen, which is visible the country around.

The three towers are: the Dagesburg of the twelfth century, and the more ancient Wekmund and the Wahlenburg, both of the eleventh century. This great ruin is the pride of the region. For breadth of horizon, pride of place and romance of lordship; for play of exquisite valley and sweep of line this stately heritage of an ancient virility really stands untranscended from Kenilworth to Heidelberg. One can hardly exaggerate its importance; dominating height and valley and poised above the quaint village nestling below, it is like unto an old imperial eagle upon its nest. If this mighty ruin is disturbed by the mine that German capitalists threaten to sink beneath its hoary walls, I can fancy uneasy stirrings in some of the many hidden tombs of the old Knights, whose war-weary bones have here rested so long in peace beneath the cross-emblazoned shields which they carried hither from the Crusades. It is said that the Roman settlers, ever envious and greedy of high places, built here their stronghold, upon the ruins of which the Knights of Eguisheim raised these mighty towers. The Romans were here, of course, long before feoffage came to occupy the region. These Romans were different men from those who succeeded them; they toiled together, man and slave, husbanding handiwork and its results for due occasion. They have left their marks all over this fair region. In the midst of thick woods one often comes across their stone altars, and the remains of their boundary walls.

They were followed by the blustering Burgraves of the Rhine, with their lavish and boasted prowess, their noisy loves and quarrels; their truculent sentimentalism, and their bloody imitation courage. Their escutcheons gave name to many a thorp hereabouts, and they held place in crusade and council, until driven out by the French, under whose rule it prospered and waxed beautiful.

French so it remained, and so it is still and always will be in spirit, no matter what befalls.

Come with me along the winding road and I will show you first a world of dark, undulating rock ground all clad in green herbage and decked with heather bells, above which hangs bristling fir. There are grassy slopes of green and gold that catch the sun. All about are hills that stand attendant, veiled in shadow for a frame. The perspective as we go along changes like a mirage, the great ruin becomes plainer, the village hides and discloses itself coquettishly; the river Laich is pretty and necessary to the picture. There are several red oxen wading in it, and one hears the sleepy pat, pat, of the washerwomen kneeling on flat stones, making soapy rings in the slow current of the stream. A drowsy fisherman leans against a tree trunk, careless of his bobbing cork. There is a sugar loaf shaped church spire, a stone wall, and a populous church yard. Sweet picture!

Now we leave this behind and climb the mount, beguiling the way with all that we can recall about the lordly owners of the castle. Perhaps in the dim past they trooped down this very path, spurring past on prancing war horse, accoutrements flashing in the morning sun, - visors, lances, chain mail all agleam. Mayhap the cohort is gathered for some festa, such as a wedding or a christening; the welcome of a stranger lord, or perhaps an act of high suzerainty is on, such as the chartering of an abbey—or an enfranchisement of Lorraine. Alliances were made here between King Henry and the Duke of Lorraine, and oaths of fealty were sworn in the great halls above on many occasions. Vows to purge the Holy Land of the paynim hordes were solemnly taken by these lords of Eguisheim, and some of these left their bones before the sacred walls. The legends are woven into the history of this great castle like a cord of scarlet. The mighty Boufflers battered at its gates, and doubtless the names of the Knights who capitulated to him are in the chronicles writ for shame in scarlet capitals by the monks. Thereafter its history is coupled with the names of brute Barons of ill repute who occupied the region when it was mangled by their hordes. Many of these wonderful old demesnes fell in such manner.

A toilsome climb brought us to a small whitewashed house, where was a very old, but bright-eyed peasant woman, who collected a fee in advance and handed us a huge key attached by a string to a long billet of wood. She then waved us away, pointing to the pathway leading through the bushes. At length we reached a beetling tower in which was a small door. Unlocking this, we came into a deep-fissured donjon with rough, jagged walls of huge stones in which were rather forbidding openings leading to subterraneans rarely explored now. Here were great heaps of debris in which were fragments of carved capitals and floriated mouldings of beautiful character. Looking upwards one saw mullions of windows, now empty of tracery, and the abutting supports of escutcheoned chimney-pieces. Here once clanked silver spurs, and rustled cloth of gold; here sparkled gems, rattled and clinked tall beakers; here oaths were sworn.

Leaning in the embrasure of one of the slender lance-like windows, one was confronted with an enchanting vista; the whole fronting gorge from foreground to distance is the castle's own. Right and left the valley rolls away and northward closes the gateway; southward is a vivid green sea of wavy table lands, and farther on one great dull green billow where another ruined castle upbears itself against a sky heavily piled with cumulus cloud.

The old custode showed us, in her hut below, a great bound volume clasped with brass and fastened by a chain to the wall. It was a manuscript register of vellum sheets minutely inscribed and here and there quaintly initialed. It seemed to be the steward's accounts of the castle, as well as I could make out, but it was in such bad repair from age, moisture and dirt that I could make little sense of it, even if I could have read it fluently, which I could not. I did, however, make out some noble names and titles, as well as statements as to the sale of cattle, and expenses for repairs. There was, too, an immense illuminated family tree, and this was folded several times, so that it was fairly in rags. Into this volume were bound a large number of sheets of paper upon which appreciative travellers had written their names and comments. I am bound to confess that we did likewise and paid the fee. And now for the legend—never mind how I had it.

The tale is told thus: In days gone by a wicked Knight Otto dwelt here, who was forever preying upon or quarrelling with the neighboring nobles. But one redeeming trait had he, according to report, in his love for his daughter, Ermintrude, who was as gentle as her sire was ill-tempered. As he was the curse of the country-side, so was she its darling pride. It chanced one day that it was reported to Otto that the Seigneur Nicolas had called him an inelegant archaic name which cannot be written here, but which may be imagined. So the very next day, when Nicolas was hunting in the forest and separated from his followers, he all at once was dragged from his horse and bound and gagged, by Otto's men, carried to Eguisheim and cast into an oubliette, where lay this doughty lord languishing for many a day upon a heap of mouldy straw, awaiting the pleasure of Otto. Came a day when, having long given himself up for very despair, he had prepared to die. All at once he heard the sound of a softly-drawn bolt, and, glancing upwards, he beheld the heavy oaken plank open, and there, all aureoled like unto a very Saint, in a flood of strong light that streamed down upon the hapless Seigneur, he looked into the sweet face of the Lady Ermintrude.

Removing the plank she stepped lightly down the rungs of the iron ladder and knelt at the side of the Seigneur Nicolas, saying, "My father is at the hunt to-day, and I am come in pity to set you free, that your blood be not upon his head," saying which she brought forth a large file and set about severing the chain at his waist, which held him fast to the wall. He, ever praying to her his thanks in broken sentences, gazed upon her lovely face, as if it had been truly that of a Holy Angel rather than that of a lovely, wilful red-cheeked maid with braided yellow hair like spun gold. So when the heavy iron band had at length been sawn through, up rose the Seigneur Nicolas painfully to his feet, and then, all at once prostrated himself at the feet of the maiden, seizing rapturously the hem of her embroidered gown and kissing it as if he would never leave off. Dirty and unkempt as he was, she thought him handsome, and with a blush she drew away, saying: "Haste—haste away! You've not an instant to lose," and Nicolas obeyed her, "but," says the chronicle, "with great reluctance, so much was he taken with her angel beauty."

Once safe away, and in his castle among his brave and doughty followers, he and they decreed that their patience with Otto being at an end, they must burn this wild boar, Otto, in his den, if they could not capture him alive. Nicolas called upon the neighboring lords for help, and they, being tired of Otto and all his works, willingly and cheerfully joined Nicolas. Early the following morning a great troop of mounted horsemen emerged upon the road leading up to the gates of Eguisheim. Among these were the high lords of Albourg, Hels, Wissen, Crey, Assembal, and Echt. At their head rode Nicolas upon a big white horse.

Otto regarded them thoughtfully from the tower window, stroking his blue-black beard with a somewhat unsteady hand, for his head still throbbed with the deep libations of the night before. Then he glowered upon his followers, "Let down the bridge," he growled, "let's see if they dare to come up—I—" What more he would have said is unknown, for he never finished. Out of the tail of his eye he caught sight of Nicolas mounted upon the great white horse, at the head of the cavalcade, —Nicolas, whom he thought safely chained by the waist to the floor of his dungeon deep below the castle walls! With a howl of anger he rushed to the court, pulled away the plank, and seizing a fire-brand threw it down into the oubliette. Of course it was empty. Then all at once the truth dawned upon him,—his daughter, Ermintrude. He rushed upon her where she stood among her women at the stairway, and dragging her away by the hair, threw her down into the dungeon where Nicolas had lain so long.

The chronicle says that he cursed them both, and that it was a long and bitter battle that was fought ere the castle was entered. But finally it was surrendered to the forces of Nicolas, the torch was put to it, and Otto—hung by the heels in chains—was about to receive the "stroke of mercy" at the hands of his conqueror, who instead said to him, "Where is Ermintrude? Tell me truly and I spare thy life, and even set thee free." But Otto, his yellow and bloodshot eyes gleaming viciously, gritted his teeth and defiantly growled out, "She is where I had thee, thou—!" "With me, warriors!" shouted Nicolas to his men; and thus into the blazing ruin of falling walls and timbers and running streams of molten lead, went the valiant Nicolas to join the fair Ermintrude, "and may their souls ever rest in Paradise." So ends the chronicle.

There is, however, it seems, another and much happier ending to this tale, which Lady Anne had from the lips of her neighbor at the table d'hôte, from whom she gathered much information regarding the region. This version had it that many years afterwards, when the old tower had been repaired and Nicolas and Ermintrude, with their children, were seated in the great court enjoying the afternoon sun, to them one day came a venerable and travel-stained old man, to beg shelter and forgiveness of those he had wronged, and that he might end his days in peace and good works in the service of God. It was the once fierce and ungodly Knight Otto, who had escaped from his captors, and gone to the Holy Land with the Crusaders, where he had been converted to Christianity. Returning thus repentant, he was welcomed by his daughter Ermintrude and forgiven by Nicolas. The tale has it that he lived long and happily with them, and was known and loved the country round for his piety and good works. Thus one may take one's choice of these endings.

The lords of this great castle were lords indeed. Paladin or Suzerain could not govern more absolutely than they. They owed allegiance only to the Emperor, and even this formed but a loose shackle that bound these marauding lords and barons to the throne. Thus the whilom lord who ruled here was at once Seigneur, Lord High Justice of provostry and town, Chief Elector, leader of all ecclesiastical officers and dignitaries, and governor in Council of State. In times of peace, when there were such, the people lived, it is gravely stated in the chronicles, "most happy and contented under such protection." Then it came to pass that ambitious Bishops and Abbots aspired to high powers. Priests overflowed the region, particularly Lotharingia (Lotharii Regnum). Great abbatial castles were built, really fortified churches; and harvests were gathered to the sound of ringing "Te Deums."

"These holy men," the Emperor Charles the Fourth is declared to have said, "no less for the renown of their virtue than for the merit of their piety, shine illustrious throughout the universe." Once the great Charlemagne, with his usual high-handedness, appeared here at one of these abbatial fortresses and amused himself by administering its offices for a period. But this form of amusement proved often the undoing of its devotees. The wearing of the mitre in the name of the cross, so attractive to ambitious nobles for its peculiar power, led to its particular punishment. In old paintings in the museums may be seen the ceremonies presided over by these ambitious princes, who wield the cross installed in all the pomp of the chair abbatial. This excited the spleen and envy of other powerful but less fortunate nobles, among them Siegfried, Count of Luxembourg, who at length induced the Emperor to turn them out, and restore the properties to the monks. The great castle and its abbey, stacked and piled with wealth and filled with countless treasures of art and precious objects brought to its treasury from age to age by both prince and pilgrim, became an object of desire, a very mine for depredation, so that again and again it was attacked and pillaged. More than once, 'tis said, in the fifteenth century, it was besieged and sacked by the Prince Archbishops of Treves, who turned it into a camp and arsenal. Albert of Brandenberg set it on fire. The Dutch troops held it for a period in the sixteenth century, levying a tax upon it of five thousand crowns in lieu of destroying it, and the sol-

diers of Louis XIV left upon its walls traces of their occupancy. Then the Revolution blasted the walls, scattered the faithful followers of the reigning baron, blew
up the great donjons, and in the smoke, fire and dust disappeared the wonderful works of art, the great library,
and all that made Dreien-Eguisheim mighty, leaving the
dismantled shell on this cliff as one now beholds it.

Türckheim

Türckheim

IT was in the plain between Colmar and Türckheim that the great Turenne surprised and defeated the Imperial German army on the 5th of January, 1675. The German forces, anticipating no battle until spring, had gone into winter quarters here, and Turenne's strategic attack, delivered with all the forces at his command, drove the Germans across the Rhine and regained Alsace.

Türckheim is now a sleepy little old walled town of about twenty-five hundred inhabitants. The little town is fairly soused in wine, for one of the very best of the vintages of Alsace is produced from its vineyards. It has a remarkable old gateway named the "Porte Basse," a creamy old stone tower, with four corbel towers, one at each corner, and a conical red tiled roof, topped with a huge ragged stork's nest. The tower is ornamented with emblazoned shields and coats of arms done in vermilion and gold, and just over the arched entrance, bearing the dates 1313–1889, is the sprawled out heraldic black eagle of Prussia—an eyesore to the loyal French inhabitants. We had intended to make our headquarters at the "Deux Clefs," but when Lady Anne beheld this lovely old gateway, with its gilded sun dial, and the quaint shadowed arch through which the peasants came and went, she decided to engage the upper room with the balcony shown at the left of my drawing. The house was named the "Storchen," and kept by a bright-eyed old lady whom I painted in the picture (frontispiece) called "Over the teacups."

Those were sunny days we spent at Türckheim, under skies as blue and clear as an awakening infant's eyes, and each and every old spire and tower a beckoning and inviting point of light. We found no other such old town as this in our wanderings; never was perhaps such a strange medley of ancient walls and turrets, dim narrow lanes and streets, rambling between high walls, where old oaken doors led into peaceful gardens all trellised and vine-clad; ancient statued Saints, rippling fountains, and the sudden cold exhalations from cask-piled cellars. We roamed these tortuous streets between amorphous houses with their aged carven doors surmounted by strange old trade emblems. Some of the houses had overhanging stories, and there were odd little buildings on rough cobbled market places where old leaden fountains trickled and wept. There was an old hall, a "Dingstuhl," they called it, where market women called out their chickens and vegetables on market day. There was, too, a small "Hospice"; an age-worn haven of rest, the gift of Ermintrude to her Saint. The Sans Culottes spared it.

TÜRCKHEIM

Although it was unusual, the Mother Superior, a most charming and dignified lady, invited Lady Anne and the writer to visit it. Behind its ivied wall was a little row of hoary dwellings; a narrow courtyard, the sacrosanct; a tiny chapel, and some contented dotards dozing and blinking in the warm sun.

In the old church the place spirit speaks at once a perfect peace, and all about the hallowed spot is tender, exuberant green, drooping its soft mantle of leaves over thronging red-tiled roofs; beyond are gardens, pastures, vineyards, 'til the plains begin their gentle slope to where, along the jagged sky line, pine spires flaunt against the blue. Whatever curious beauty is in old gables, whatever charm one can find in valuing them, is here to be found to the last degree.

On the other side of the valley there is a charming little village called Winzenheim, above which is the ancient remains of the castle of Hohlandsburg, now consisting of little more than a vast heap of stones covered with beflowered vines. There is also, or was in 1910, a most delightful if somewhat down-at-heel Inn, mismanaged by one Monsieur Keeler-Beeler, who there calmly pursued the even tenor of his high-minded existence all unmoved by events, while the world rolled 'round, surveying all happenings whatsoever with untroubled mind, elevated brows and cynic eye; who shrugged his shoulders at the demands of the uniformed tax collector, yet handed over clinking coin unemotionally, at least as far as one could judge of his feelings. This cynic eye encompassed the writer seated on the vine-clad small balcony, the afternoon of our arrival by malle-post. After an interval of silent, bovine-like gaze which penetrated, passed through me and enveloped Lady Anne, who appeared in the window behind,—he removed his hat and asked: "Would 'Mossié,' and the Gracious Madame compliment him by tasting the famous 'Rangener'?"—adding that its flavor is never to be forgotten. We would, and did. He was right, too.

At this Inn dwelt in amity a small coterie of painters who, we were told, came here year after year, for love of the region. I do not know anything of their industry in art,—they seemed not to toil, but they certainly were always promptly in their places when our host rang the dinner gong. Four francs fifty a day, everything included, held them here hugging their chains. Why not? —when there were to be had such omelettes! such fish!— and occasionally a glass of the never to be forgotten "Rangener." Four days the spell held us, and Lady Anne skilfully extracted a legend of the mountain from the taciturn inn-keeper. It seems that high upon the top of the Mount, where sprawls the misshapen ruin of Hohlandsburg is, or was, a little old hermitage cut out of the solid rock. Once upon a time, in the days of the Romans, a certain holy eremite dwelt here in piety and poverty. His name was Postumius (or something like it), and for a companion he had a pet hare, to which he was devoted. With it he shared his frugal meals, and by night it lay beside him upon his poor bed of leaves and moss. In those days there was here in the valley a great Monastery, presided over by a Holy Abbot. One dark and stormy night this Abbot sent for a young monk, and as penance for some infraction of the rules of the monastery, ordered him to climb the Hohlandsburg to the hermit's cave in all the wind and rain, and bring back with him the hermit's cord, worn about his waist, as evidence that he had accomplished the task.

The young monk—he was hardly more than a novice —set out obediently, and after a long and wearisome toil, reached the hermit's cave after midnight. The holy man was absent upon some mission of mercy, but the door was open, and there, lying upon the rude pallet, was the pet hare. The young monk entered and sitting down on the pallet, snapped his fingers at the gentle beast, which confidingly went to him and climbed into his lap, thinking no evil of a young monk. The youth caressed it and it lay there contentedly. An hour passed, in which he twice trimmed the rude oil lamp that burned beside the pallet, casting flickering and wavering strangely shaped shadows on the earthen walls and rock ceiling of the cave. All was silent but the rush of the wind. All suddenly the Spirit of Evil entered into the young monk; he whipped out his knife and cut off one of the poor hare's soft paws, which the devil persuaded him was what the Abbot wished him to bring back to the monastery. Flinging the poor bleeding hare upon the pallet, he set off in the darkness down the winding, rocky and dangerous path to the valley below.—He was never seen afterwards.

When the holy hermit returned in the morning he found the poor hare sitting patiently upon the pallet, holding up a still bleeding stump. Filled with grief and great compassion, the hermit bound up the wound with simple herbs, after which he bade the animal go seek its missing paw. The hare limped away down the stony pathway to the valley, where it circled unceasingly about the great monastery walls, regularly appearing at the gateway and begging for admission, but although the watchman on the tower saw the small beast coming and going, and sitting up on its haunches holding the wounded paw so that it might be plainly seen, it never occurred to him that it was other than a tame hare strayed from the village, and he gave it no heed. So, unable to gain admittance, the poor animal limped away and returned to the hermit. But in the meantime that aged holy man, exhausted by his long vigils and his privations, had succumbed to the rigors of the stormy night, and lay dead upon the pallet of leaves in the cave. To him crept the poor hare, who, failing to rouse his beloved master, lay down beside him and died. Since then, these many hundred years, on one certain night of the year when it usually storms, and the rain beats down upon old Hohlandsburg, the poor hare may be seen by whomsoever is out on the road, limping along over the stony way, seeking her missing paw. "As for me," concluded the innkeeper, "of course, I have not seen her myself, but many of the old inhabitants will tell Madame that they have of a surety seen the limping hare of Hohlandsburg, and who shall say that they are untruthful?"

This legend of the hare has several variations; here is another of perhaps greater picturesqueness: "In the tenth century, when the holy and learned Theofrid governed the abbey and by his example made all to venerate him, there dwelt in a vast cavern on the mountain top, the exact location of which is now unknown, a very terrible old magician and sorcerer of most dreadful mien, called Schlattzele or Spattzele, one or the other. His only purpose in life was to illtreat those who come near him. And should no one come near him, he would go in pursuit of a victim. He hated all men, but particularly monks and holy men, because Theofrid had regenerated the people throughout the region and saved their souls from perdition.

"Thus through this magician, misfortune fell upon one after the other of the God-fearing and industrious farmers of the region. Their cattle sickened and died;

their crops, when ready for the harvest, were mysteriously attacked by blight, or when harvested laboriously, were burned in the night. The vineyards were ruined by avalanches of stones, which descended during storms and obliterated them. The bending fruit trees were up-rooted by fierce windstorms and howling hurricanes, under cover of darkness, and the peaceful, winding river rose, bursting its banks, and flooded the level fields, sweeping away farmsteads and drowning the cattle. Fevers attacked the people, who died of them despite the simples and prayers of the monks. And finally appeared wild beasts and fierce bands of wolves, who devoured the sheep and even carried off women and children.

"So the people came to the abbey asking the holy Theo-frid to intercede in their behalf, that they might be deliv-ered from this terrible curse which had fallen upon them. So Theofrid prayed unto the Lord, not for himself, but for his people, that they might be delivered from the curse. And he named the name of the sorcerer. And the Lord harkened unto Theofrid, who did not pray for himself, or for his monks, but for his people. And He delivered the people from the curse of the sorcerer, so that they had peace thereafter. But the evil sorcerer did then turn his entire attention upon the holy Theofrid and did torment him grievously.

"All at once a great black, hairy animal, in form like unto a cat, haunted the cell of the holy man while he was at prayer. How it entered was impossible to say, but bolts and bars hindered it not. This beast would walk about the kneeling Theofrid, with tail erect, purring softly and often rubbing against the terrified man. He found it impossible to fix his mind upon his prayers, for the most terrible, and hideous, and sinful thoughts filled his mind. Even at holy mass the words he uttered were often not those of the sacred office, but diabolical chants and exorcisms took their place. And often in the middle of the night he heard the sound of rubbing and soft pushing against the barred door of his cell, so he was compelled to cover his ears that he might not hear, for he was strangely impelled to arise and open the door.

"He realized that he was being bewitched. For in the great chained book kept in the abbey, all fairly written by the monkish chronicler, was a tale of black art, and also the means of overcoming it. And he studied this book and mastered it, so that he knew it well, for Theofrid was a man of parts, and skill, and resource. Kneeling down one morning at daybreak in his cell, after a night spent in terror and resistance, he prayed unto the Lord for assistance, and then he rose from his knees in resolve. That night he fastened one end of a strong, fine cord into a cunning noose, and this he placed just outside his door on the stone flagging and waited. In the middle of the night he heard again the sounds of purring and the rubbing of a soft body against the door. Theofrid, reciting the exorcism, seized the cord and gave it a firm, quick pull; he felt the noose tighten and heard the "thud" of a heavy body. Then he gave a mighty pull at the cord and there came a horrid scream, and then another, sounding farther away; finally these cries ceased. Theofrid opened the door and there in the noose he found a bloody, hairy paw cut completely off above the joint. Theofrid built a huge fire, in which he burned the paw, and scattered the ashes to the winds, as was right and proper under such a circumstance. For the directions in books of magic specifically state that in case you mutilate a horrid magician or sorcerer, you must destroy the part with fire, for he cannot then by his black art get back his human form until you restore to him the part of which you deprived him, and thus he ever after remains in the guise which he assumed to do you ill. Of course then, Theofrid, knowing that, did as I have related, and the sorcerer, deprived of his power for evil doing, so it is said, in the form of a limping, glowering beast, still slinks about the mountain top, trying to find the bones of his missing foot."

Here in this mountainous region all is different from the gentler southern hills and valleys, for these are the dim pine-clad forests, in which the sturdy peasantry fought the usurper for the right to be French and remain so. These old towns and villages cluster about the castle and abbey-crowned crags, embayed in the sweeping, faultless crescents of gleaming streams, and each approached from either side by long parabolas of lush green valley and meadow.

The peculiar charm of these Alsatian village nests lies in their curving, vine-clad, creamy-walled streets and lanes. In some of them the huddled houses lie in deep natural trenches below the castles' grim walls, and the streets curve naturally with the river's curve. From these walls one looks down upon the crescent of peaceful homesteads, from which blended sounds float upward to the ear; the tinkle of a smith's hammer, the chatter of birds, the soft lowing of distant oxen, all merged, as Lady Anne poetically expressed it, like unto the muffled melody in a sea shell. These towns and villages are draped monuments to the loyalty of the Alsace-Lorrainers. When the usurper annexed these provinces, he took instant measures to reduce the hapless inhabitants to a condition compared with which feudal vassalage had its advantages. Not only was personal liberty and opinion suppressed, but upon their sacred customs was imposed the shadow of the Prussian eagle. On these mountain slopes was enacted an agonizing drama. Families were uprooted and fled across the frontier, leaving comfort for penury and privation. Terrible stories of this period are still related by the peasants on both sides of the border.

One Alsatian patriot of 1871 is said to have escaped

to a forest, where he discovered a large hollow tree into which he descended. When after a period he fancied his pursuers gone, and the way clear, he tried to climb out, but found that the sides sloped upwards and there was nothing which offered purchase to hand or foot. There he remained famished. He shouted for help as loudly as he could, but no help came. When the peasants heard him they thought of evil spirits in the wood and hastened away from the spot in terror. For days, then, the unfortunate man must have shouted for the help that never came. "Only last year," said my informer, "the 'Schlitteurs' (wood cutters) cut down the great hollow tree and found huddled in the cavity at its base a mouldered skeleton, the fragments of a French gun, and a small sum of silver and copper money."

Thann

Thann

AT the mouth of the narrow valley of the Thur, where the dark-wooded mountains enclose it with heavy forests above and smiling golden vineyards in the slopes below, is Thann. On the left bank of the river the ruin of a great castle crowns the wooded hill-top, commanding the busy town, the winding river, crossed by two bridges, and the entrance to the valley. This great ruin is the Engelburg, which was destroyed by Turenne in the year 1674, and now resembles somewhat the bulk of a huge cask, or the base of a great stool, used by a gray old giant who gathered his worldly goods about him on the hilltop and there sat during the attack. In truth it was a stronghold long before the lord of Engelburg (Angel's Fortress) seized the site for his castle. The Roman settlers, ever covetous of high places, "Épris des hauteurs," built a fortress and refuge there long before feoffage arrived. They were higher men than any that came after, and, trusting in their wary eyes, husbanded hand's toil and body's sweat for due occasion. There are ancient Roman Gallic names all over the Province, along the water sheds marking off the

233

tribal borders and boundaries. After these came the blustering burgraves with their lavish prowess, noisy loves and hates, and blood-thirsty sentimentalism, and from these were named each overhanging thorp.

Coming down by the zigzag road one sees: at first a world of dark undulating rock land in vesture of shining green herbage and heather-bells, high bordered with the bristling fir, deep girdled across with a devious stream. Petty detail of feature is lost in largeness. Little by little, as one descends, the picture narrows until the castle looms into frowning focus, cresting with an armory of spikey green wrack its mountain cone. From this descends a fall of grassy slopes that catch the sun and glow with its gilding. Each step changes the view and obliterates the last.

A pillared Saint in a weatherbeaten wooden pent seems out of place amid such wildness, mossy thatch and winding honeysuckle seek to hide it; then the long, low valley carpet; the level, decorous river with peaceful oxen grazing or wading; the sleepy pit-pat-pat of women washing clothes at the river edge, kneeling in quaint wooden boxes; a few people passing on the nearest bridge, and an angler below lolling half awake, propped up in the stern of an anchored punt,—this is the picture. One may close one's eyes to the factory chimneys, if one is so minded, and forget them. Likewise may he ignore most of the seventy-eight hundred population should they perchance not interest him. They will object not at all.

One may linger near the winding mountain paths and there beguile his days with necromancy, raising the lordly ghosts of the Barons of Engelburg in imagination so that they come trooping down the stony way spurring past on prancing horse, breastplate flashing and chain mail rattling, on the way to some "festa," maybe the wedding of the Lady Ermintrude or the banquet of Wenceslas; the triumphant return of the Duke of Lorraine, or Philip's celebration of the oath of fealty. Or maybe they are on their way to Strassburg to the Tourney, where there is call for much skill of arm and eagle eye.

Throughout the region the story of Engelburg runs like a scarlet cord in the tapestry, but later on all this pattern of tapestry is worn, faded, and ravelled into a gray rag, and the Seigneurie has passed into careless hands. Barons and Knights came and went in the ages. It passed through sieges; warriors attacked it patiently and were received by the ensconced Baron with showers of hot lead, ancient offal, and such other confetti as they could contrive at intervals between the launching of stone balls, and showers of iron bolts. Engelburg held out with doglike persistence to the end, until they threw their redoubts against the ravine and gave him such a battering that at last he appeared on the ramparts and gave in. Most of these strongholds, deemed so long impregnable, tottered and fell like ninepins when shot at with French powder and cannon. Many indeed disappeared with scarcely a trace when the stones were overgrown with ivy. One passes between walls that seem more than ten feet thick, where Seigneural lodge, donjon, and keep still stand all moss grown, and there are the arches of Knights' hall, and above is what was "my lady's chamber," with crumbling stone seat in the narrow window wherein she must have sat in days long gone, and gazed out over the golden slopes, the valley, and the winding white road. One lingers here until the splashes of golden light are gone from the valley, and a vapory canopy of rose shot lilac envelops the setting of the sun.

There was a huge circular ragged mass of masonry on the hilltop, resembling somewhat the end of a great spool set up side-ways as if overturned by a giant hand. It is called here the "Eye of the Sorcerer," and is the object of much superstition by the peasants. A little maid was leaning against its side, but when she saw us she fled away down the rough path, and nothing would induce her to return. But in the sketch which I made, I placed her just where she stood to complete the picture. It was certainly a wild looking spot, and the "Sorcerer's Eye" was well placed, for sitting in the great round hole we had a magnificent view of the dim luminous valley which well repaid us for the climb. There must have been some sort of a legend connected with the "Eye," but what it was I must confess with some shame we never discovered, although we questioned repeatedly those old people whom we fancied could satisfy us. Strange sights and sounds have been met with here of nights, for, so they say, this venerable height harbors gruesome things: that sorcerers foregathered here aforetime, and they also say, do even now hector those who would pry into the secrets of the past.

When the ancient ruins of the monastery suppressed by Joseph II, whoever he was, were made over into a factory, the place was haunted, o'nights, by pranksome, ill-natured spooks. According to the story of mine entertaining host, related to Lady Anne one time I was absent sketching the Sorcerer's Eye, the factory master's life was made a burden to him. When his dinner was laid for him, and his wife went to call him, the platters, cups and bottles were thrown about the room in all directions. Some wiseacre advised him to shoot silver bullets into the room to the accompaniment of appropriate exorcism. This, however, not only proved too expensive, but failed to produce any result, so old horse shoe nails were tried; again without effect. Then the expedient of strewing the floor with wood ashes was tried, in the hope that these might discourage the witch or goblin, for by some reason known in this region, such folk either dislike the ashes of wood, or are unable to cross a threshold so strewn—

accounts differ. But, related mine host to Lady Anne, these strewn ashes revealed the next morning some tell-tale footprints—leading to a disused closet. Whereupon the factory master loaded the blunderbuss to the muzzle with old nails and scrap, and under the eye of the Mayor, all clad in his sash of office for the occasion, did then and there discharge it at the closet door, when in it fell, and out there tumbled the body of a man, who proved to be a fellow formerly employed as clerk by the master, whom he had discharged for stealing, and who had taken this means of avenging himself. The body was buried in a pit filled with lime at night in the marsh below the Sorcerer's Eye, and, continues the story,—on stormy nights, etc., etc.

Mine host, under further encouragement, told a better one of a Demon who still rocks children's cradles, in which are babies under the age of six months, should the mother or nurse for an instant leave them unattended —rocks them so hard that the babes perish in convulsions! This happened to such an extent as to alarm the towns-people; twelve children thus perished. So the wise woman of the village adopted the simple expedient of removing the rockers from all the cradles, "which," gravely alleged mine host, the while avoiding my eye, "baffled the evil spirit, and since then he has not left the summit of the hill." Somehow, I cannot rid myself of the impression that mine host was "stringing" us! . . .

THANN

The huge mass of masonry so curiously balanced on the hilltop, is, according to Erckmann-Chatrian, the remains of the top of the great tower of the castle of Engelsburg, which after the treaty of Westphalia (1648) passed with the town of Thann over to Cardinal Mazarin. Afterwards at the order of Turenne, Pedro de Poncet appealed to the miners of Giromagny to blow up and destroy the old castle. Three times, and unsuccessfully, did they make the attempt. The first resulted in the overthrow of the manor walls; on the second attempt the donjon sank to half its height; and on the third a huge section comprising this great ring turned up on its side, and remains the wonder of the country side.

The inn was entirely delightful. Each afternoon the noise of ninepins sounded from the rear garden, where grave burghers were gathered at the game, and it was difficult for the landlord to induce them to come to the dinner of unexceptionable cutlets, souffle and a generous bottle of the "Rangener" wine, extolled as far back as 1550. . . . In days thereafter we explored the region, discovering by chance a spring that is said to be far famed for the cure of rickets and such like complaints in children, and to which yearly come priests in solemn procession bringing with them crowds of pilgrims, who lave their children with the waters, leaving small wooden crosses and such like "ex voto" in gratitude. There is great faith in this water, we were told. Its origin is lost

in the dim ages. But a village priest related that in
early days the Roman Fontanalia were celebrated hereabouts, and thus this and other springs were venerated.
The Danish Saint Pirminus preached the gospel throughout Lorraine, so his name is still used to qualify certain
ailments common to children, and his effigy is seen in the
wayside chapels.

It was our fortune to come upon a celebration of the
Kermis, where were gathered bevies of pretty fair-haired
girls with full-laced bosoms, and attentive young fellows
garbed in quaint, high-waisted, many-buttoned coats,
who paraded the flag hung streets, shyly holding hands.

And we were forced against the wall to let the "Malle-
post" pass, a huge sort of diligence, archaically painted
in yellow, with a long body and many small windows,
four huge wheels, and a set of brakes, in protection
against steep descents, made of two old top boots of incredible size on each rear wheel. The whole ark was
drawn by six powerful horses. We thought that it might
be good fun to go on by this to the next town, and as
Lady Anne was agreed we mounted to the interior by
means of the steep steps at the rear door. Presently
appeared the burly driver, the leading horses were
brought out, and then came a crowd of peasants who
precipitated themselves into the old ark, which swayed
and rocked with their entry. Each peasant was laden
with one or two bundles which he bestowed as best he

might, regarding us not at all. Then, amid boisterous laughter and shouts, and with many handshakings through the door and open windows, we started. Ere we had gone a square the diligence stopped and in got four more peasants with bundles. At another square another pair demanded place, and room was made for them too. This continued at intervals until we reached the edge of the town, and the old ark, which was designed to accommodate sixteen, eight on each lengthwise seat, held twenty-two. Crushed and rigidly held on either side by these full bodied lusty peasants, we speculated as to what would happen to us if two more were added to the number, all of whom were seated on the two benches; eleven on each! when lo! the ark again stopped and two more entered the door. Happily these were children, who secured seats on some of the bundles on the floor among the feet. Thus we journeyed as far as the Staufen, about a mile and a half beyond the town, which we reached in safety. Here the driver demanded a mark each for our "places," and we bade good-by to the twenty-two smiling, good-natured, squeezed ones, and away they went out of our ken forever.

Thann entertained us very well indeed. There is a real gem of Gothic architecture there in the church of St. Theobald, the choir of which may be seen from the station, and dates from 1351–1421. It has a bold and most elegant open tower, the work of Meister Remigius

Walch (1516) whose name is said to be carved on the spire, but I could not find it. There is also a handsome double portal on the west side. The interior is lavishly adorned with ornamentation and carving of the sixteenth century. The stained glass windows are very satisfying, and over the altar there is a fine example of the work of Martin Schongauer, showing the Saviour surrounded by the Apostles. There are also many most picturesque old towers, houses with gardens, and rows of tall poplars on the river, of which I made a sketch.

Rosheim

Rosheim

ERE was a little town with houses all embowered in roses and vines, which well merited its name. It is said to have more than three thousand inhabitants, but one wonders where they kept themselves; certainly not more than a score or two were visible the day we spent there; the streets were deserted, and the table d'hôte at the good little inn brought forth only one other guest besides ourselves, he a melancholy looking and seedy "commis voyageur," who rarely lifted his eyes from his plate, and ate noisily from the point of his knife. The inn was named the "Pflug." That however was the only thing against it.

Rosheim was once *a free city* of the Empire, whatever that may mean, and it is said to have been sacked and burned repeatedly in now forgotten wars. There were still some of the ancient fortifications standing in good preservation, and there was a remarkable old gateway with a strange peaked roof of slate set in diamond pattern, and on its wall a large clock-face, painted white, with black figures. At each side were quaintly-gabled houses with wooden balconies belonging to a remote period.

Before the gate was a fountain of stone raised on three steps, with a "baldaquin," where women and girls filled their pails. The rest of the town seemed silent and deserted. We explored the old Romanesque Church of SS. Peter and Paul, said to have been consecrated in the year 1049. It has a great octagonal tower with a pointed conical slate roof, which in spite of its ugliness was most impressive from its massive size. We happened upon a large courtyard, with wide open doors at its farther end, and these framed a charming picture. On the farther side was an open sort of "grenier," its broken bars standing out all golden in the sunlight against deep ultramarine shadows within. Beside it, a flight of crumbling mossy steps led up to the garden shadowed by a huge tree; gay nasturtium blossoms clothed the top of the wall, and some blue and white garments were hanging there to dry. Here among the gold-flecked straw under the "grenier" a group of hens and chickens scratched about a lordly "Monsieur le Coq."

It was here that we fell in with the mountebank dentist and his daughter. A wagon was drawn up beside the wall: a strange-looking vehicle, something like those pictures one sees of the old *diligences* which were in use before the railways. This one was painted red, green and blue. It looked like a house on wheels, having three

246

doors, one to each of the front compartments, and one for the back, where a sort of ladder was fixed. The horse had been taken out, the shafts raised, with a stake supporting them, and the horse turned about between them, facing the seat, where he munched contentedly at a measure of hay. A door opened and out came a fantastically dressed girl, followed by two small black dogs, who jumped and cavorted about her. We followed to a small stream, where she busied herself washing a pair of shoes with a brush and soap. The two dogs barked at us furiously, resenting our presence. The girl wore a fantastic sort of velvet cap, covered with gold stars of tinsel. I ventured to ask her if those were performing dogs. She shook her head and replied: "No M'sieur, they are my pets. No, we are not circus people, as you imagine. My father is a man of science. We live in the wagon—it is our house. We travel thus while my father practices his profession. He is a dentist. We are French, and we come from Paris. Is M'sieur not English? Ah, —American. And what language does M'sieur speak? —English— Well then, how is it that M'sieur *speaks* English, but he is American—I do not understand—"

All at once a loud, harsh voice behind us broke in:

"Nom d'Dieu, imbecile! thou art spoiling my shoes and wasting good soap, too."

Close beside us was the most villainous-looking man I had ever seen, glaring at the girl, who cowered before him. There were traces of powder and rouge upon her poor white withered face; she could not have been much more than nineteen or twenty, yet she looked older. Her eyes beneath the frizzled sandy bang of faded hair looked as if she had cried away their youthful brightness.

The man switched viciously at the ground with a whip which he carried, much as if he would have used it on her had we not been there. We walked on, but, looking back, saw him standing over her threateningly, still scolding.

He quite spoiled the scene for us, this serpent in the garden. The green strip of meadow, the clear river murmuring over its flat stones; and across, the osier-shaded road stretching towards the dark fringe of trees. Warm sunshine glowed over all, and the grass and leaves shone with all the freshness brought by the morning's showers, and yet for us all the sweet charm of its perfect repose had gone from that lovely spot, while that fierce-eyed sallow-faced man stood there threatening the shrinking girl.

In the afternoon the loud beating of a drum was heard, and we followed a few of the villagers, coming at length upon the dentist's painted wagon, which had been moved to a more public spot.

Upon the very top of the wagon was the girl, now dressed in a gorgeous crimson robe, furiously beating a large bass drum, while the dentist, dressed in a black

velvet waistcoat and knee breeches and in his shirt
sleeves, a spotless white frilled shirt with huge cuffs, its
bosom sparkling and gleaming with large gold studs,
stood on the small seat in front. He took off a great
cocked hat which he wore on his head, and waved it with
some grace at the people who stood about. To him
climbed a man in a blue blouse, who whispered something
to him with evident anxiety. The dentist hesitated for
an instant and then bawled out: "Yes—Yes—Certainly
—be calm—be easy—do not trouble—I shall come to
your house in a short time—about an hour—rest easy, all
will be well!" The man got down and went away.
"And now, good people," said he, turning to the villagers
who stood open-mouthed before him, "you wish to know
what 'tis all about? Eh! Well, I promise you certain
wonders—hear me and treasure my words, for I bring you
health, and science, and comfort! You will say, who is
this who has come here among us from the far off great
city of Paris. Does this man come to deceive us?—to
take our money from us? By no means, my friends. I
come here not to sell you anything—but to give away my
wonderful medicine—free—free as the air and water!
Look"—and he held up a small jar. "This pot holds a
miracle—one small pinch of this ointment—only as
much as would go on the point of a spoon—has already
to-day here produced a remarkable cure, and yet of this
wonderful healing balm I am going to give freely—to

any of you who are ailing—come up and show me your stiff arm or leg—or your aching back—come to me and be cured! Free—for nothing!"

Then he opened a sort of box before him—and showed glass jars in which were frogs and bugs floating in spirit. The girl on the roof at each period banged the great drum. The peasants eyed him and each other, evidently impressed by his offer of free treatment, but were still suspicious.

"You say to yourselves," went on the mountebank, "'this professor claims that he has a remedy for every and all diseases—an infallible remedy!' You are wrong! I did not claim that! I have here a remedy," he held up the little jar with one hand, and with the long lean, yellow forefinger of the other he pointed at each of his hearers, "a remedy, not for every disease, but"—a longer pause—"for *some* diseases—and for these"—pause—"it is surely infallible!" Bang! went the drum.

"There are ailments about which I do not concern myself. I might possibly cure them, or then again I might not." (Bang.) "I never tried." (Bang.) "I cure twelve maladies of humankind." (Bang.) "The first is cancer." (Bang.) "The second is consumption of the lungs." (Bang.) "The other ten I explain in private to my patients." (Bang.) "Among these is rheumatism." (Bang.)

One old peasant who stood beneath him here produced a silver coin and held it up to the quack.

"Look," said he, pointing down to the old fellow. "He has faith." (Bang.) "Admire him, for he is no fool!—Nay, my friend," he continued, "I shall not take your money—but you shall come to me by and by and tell me what ails you, and then you may be sure, if my wonderful remedy is for your ailment, you shall have it." (Bang.)

By this time we had had quite enough of all this, and we came away. He probably fleeced the people well, for he departed during the night. Maybe there was a story connected with him and the poor faded girl, who may or may not have been his daughter. Perhaps even he appeared to be more villainous and evil than he really was, or why should she stay with him? But he certainly looked capable of any sort of crime.

Metz

Metz

ONE might seek in vain to find a town more distinctly French than Metz, the fortified capital of Lorraine and before the present war the headquarters of the 16th army corps, numbering about twenty-six thousand soldiers, and with a population of about seventy thousand, of which about one-half are French.

Approaching the town by rail one sees upon the horizon, high above the roofs and towers, two huge squat, green constructions, which seem entirely out of place, and are ugly beyond expression. One turns out to be the great gas tank built by the Germans on "Serpenoise" plain; the other is the roof of the huge railway station, which is quite as ugly, but much more offensive, because it claims to be architecture. Says M. Emile Hinzelin,[1] describing it, "On the tower which surmounts this depot an immense block of yellow stone was long an enigma to us. It at length turned out to be Saint George and the Dragon. At least that is what the Germans alleged it to be, adding, insultingly, that it represented the German Empire treading under foot the French Republic. The

[1] Directeur de "La France de Demain" (Alsace-Lorraine).

Administration substituted another model for this, without giving an explanation for the change of plan. This model included the figure of Field Marshal Count Hoeseler, a Corps Commander of the army of Metz. Imagine," continues he, "a man who at fifty paces resembles a child disguised as a soldier; at twenty, a petty officer; at ten, an ugly old woman! In Hoeseler is incarnated the effigy of the traditional Superior Officer, such as is typified by the grim mask-like face of von Moltke. But what an idea it was to represent Hoeseler as Roland in a buckler and coat of mail! At the same time one should not be astonished at this lack of taste, for is there not sculptured on the doorway of the Cathedral an effigy of the Emperor William (made on Imperial command) in the costume and with the attributes of the Prophet Daniel!"

One could hardly believe this to be true, but true it is,—the acme of banality! There it stands in the present west portal. That lovely piece of Gothic work which was sculptured in the eighteenth century by Blondel was demolished by the German administration, who gravely reported that Blondel's style did not agree with or carry out the original plans of the architects of the Cathedral. The removal of this master work of Blondel's was nothing short of a crime. And one is led to believe and accept the explanation of the French architects who protested against the substitution, "That it was really because Blondel was a Frenchman." This original west portal was presented by Louis XV as a votive offering for his recovery from the illness which attacked him during the singing of the "Te Deum" at the celebration of the taking of Château-Dauphin by the army of Piedmont. This wretched neo-Gothic construction was inaugurated with much pomp and ceremony in May, 1903. It is a conglomeration the like of which is enough to turn the gorge of any architect or student—and all at once one sees the crowning offence in the figure labeled "Daniel the Prophet," holding in its left hand a scroll to which the right points.

The hooded head is lifted, and from it looks forth the face of the German Emperor, upturned moustache—confident smile, and all those unmistakable points of visage with which we have become so accustomed in the daily prints. This bizarre portal may be seen at the left hand corner of my drawing faintly sketched—purposely so—because it is so ugly and entirely out of keeping with its surroundings. It should be the duty of the French Ministry of Fine Arts to remove it as soon as the German occupancy is at an end, and I have no doubt this will be done.

The Cathedrals of Metz and Strassburg are in striking contrast. The latter is so tall of tower, so sombre upon the horizon; and this impression is enhanced at closer view. Metz, on the contrary, not lacking a flèche, but without a high tower, is more exquisite in style. The people of Metz are most enthusiastic about it. "Have you not seen our magnificent stained glass?" they ask, and then, "Ah, but Monsieur must see it at night from the square outside when it is lighted." The artists call it "The casket filled with roses and breathing incense." The common people speak of it as "the holy lantern." We are told that in this Cathedral are four thousand and seventy-four square metres of painted glass, and that those in the south aisle are of the thirteenth century, while those in the nave, the transept and the choir are of the fourteenth, fifteenth and sixteenth centuries respectively.

The slender tower at the side is of exquisite proportion and is finished by a beautiful flèche, a veritable chef d'œuvre of carving. From its platform one can see Trèves to the north, and to the south and west the towers of some of the French towns. In the tower is a great bell, named The Mute, which has an inscription "Je suis la pour crier Justice." It is a matter of record that it rang steadily for two days and nights in October, 1870.

Outside of Metz is a very picturesque village of small white houses, with delightful red tiled roofs lost here and there among the thick foliage of large trees. But the extraordinary thing about it is the gigantic chain of arcades, in ruins here and there, with immense upstanding pillars towering over the small white houses in the fields and orchards. These are the remains of a Roman aqueduct which crosses the valley. The little town huddling below is called Jouy-aux-Arches, and is given over to the cultivation of strawberries, of which it, and three other fully as quaint villages named respectively Woippy, Saulny, and Lorry, ship each year something like five hundred thousand kilograms of the berries to market, not to speak of the other fruits grown, such as apricots, cherries, peaches and prunes. On the left bank of the Moselle near Woippy is grown a very delicate and noble grape, which produces a wine of remarkable bouquet. There are also the wines of Scy, of Jussy, of Sainte Ruffine and Rozerieulles, each of which has its admirers. Many of the villages hereabouts retain their French names only in the hearts of the Alsatian people, for following the forcible annexation Thionville became Diedenhoffen; Sarreguemines became Saargmund; Boulay, Bolchen; and so on ad nauseam. Imagine charming little Devant-les-ponts masquerading as "Fanttlesspountt"!

Metz itself has had a remarkable history. The Divodurum of the Romans, it was afterwards the chief fortified town of the Gallic tribe called the Mediomatrici. A Bishop was enthroned there in the fourth century, and subsequently it became the capital of the Kingdom of the Austrasians under their first King Theodoric. The remains of his palace are still to be seen in the rue Trinitaires, where some fragments and stones are shown. It was a free city until taken by the French in 1552, and was successfully defended by its inhabitants and the French soldiers against Charles V. Together with Toul and Verdun it was governed as part of France, and so remained until the Germans seized it in 1871. One hardly knows where to begin or where to stop in writing of the history of Metz, so filled with interest and great events are the chronicles.

Let us include a little of the Revolution. In June, 1790, the National Guard of Lorraine, Alsace and Franche-Comte were convoked at Strassburg. The Mayor of Strassburg, Frederic Dietrich, at whose house the "Marseillaise" was first sung by its young author, Rouget de l'Isle, came officially to receive the flag of the nation, the tri-color, which he hoisted on the platform of the Cathedral, saying, "I thus show to Germany that the Empire of Liberty is founded in France." This patriotic ceremony of hoisting the flag was afterwards repeated on the Cathedral at Metz, in the presence of the Guard. Hereafter it was truly the Empire of Liberty—Liberty of action and men.

For the defense of the land there came into existence an army of heroic men among whom the names of Bouchotte, Lasalle, Custine and Richepause are ever wreathed in glory. The people of Alsace-Lorraine were among those who took the Bastille. The tri-color was

their banner. Its traditions and its glories were theirs.
The old citadel, constructed by Marshal Vielleville, in
1562 was reconstructed by Vauban, who made of Metz
a splendid fortified town. He conceived the work as a
means toward peace, saying, "Fortresses should have no
other end than the preservation of life." Thereafter
Asfeld and Cormontaigne carried out the original plans
of Vauban in building the other ramparts.

Outside forts were built by the government following
Sadowa, at Philippeville, Saint-Quentin, Saint Julian,
Saint Privat and Queulen, and this work was carried on
up to the war of 1870. When Metz fell into the hands
of the Germans they continued and completed this work
of defense, but they were animated by a different thought
and purpose. It was not simply defense that they
thought of, but domination. They made of Metz a
great war machine which was to be ever ready against
the time when they should be ready to launch against
France an irresistible army of invasion. It is shown that
up to 1900 the perimeter of plan was not more than
twenty five kilometres. When the great war of 1914
broke out, the fortifications embraced seventy five kilometres. . . . All the works between the Rhine and Metz
were connected by a series of strategical roads and railways connected by subterranean telephones. They destroyed and obliterated the ancient fortifications as useless for the defence of the town, leaving only Fort Belle-

croix, which they named Steinmetz. This latter com-
mands the railway. The town became a vast arsenal.
Travellers in 1913 returning to France reported that two
army corps had been sent to Metz to man the ramparts,
and that at Saarbruck was another numbering twenty
thousand men. The world gave no heed to these preparations. . . .

The work of Germanizing the architecture of the town
went on merrily. Near the atrociously Teutonic railway station, they built a huge Post Office, a sort of cross
between a jail and a church, covered with bizarre bas-
reliefs and topped with a kind of balloon of iron work.
A Frenchman wittily described the ornamentation as
looking like "the mud pie work of a child, all gilded by
a cook's assistant." In 1906 the ancient picturesque
ramparts were leveled. They must have been a remarkable setting for the town, and there was really no need
of destroying them, but with that curious blindness of
the Germans to what constitutes real beauty and value,
they proceeded to remove what were regarded as historical monuments and replaced them with rows of modern (!) houses so fantastic and bizarre as to be almost
unbelievable, and of no one recognizable style, but a
conglomeration of all. Some of these houses seem to
have broken out into a sort of rash of balconies, and are
festooned with baroque cast iron work. Others are lined
with columns which do not serve to support any part of

the design. There are tall slender windows and wide squatty ones, in what is termed "Art Nouveau" style (!) There is German Renaissance carried out to the extreme, and there is what they call Gothic, and all is mixed up in a terrible jumble violating every known rule of architecture.

The roofs are of tile in every color of the rainbow, each in its crudest tone, and all entirely out of harmony with everything. In contrast to these offences against taste, one turns to the contemplation and enjoyment of the ancient French façades of the periods of Louis XIV, and XVI, their elegant lines and proportions proving an antidote for the suffering caused by the wretched houses near the station. Some of the ancient towers happily still remain, though just why they were spared when the lust of tearing down took place it is hard to say.

Formerly, it is said, one entered the town passing through the ancient gateway "Porte Serpenoise," called now by the Germans, "Prinz Friedrich Karl Thor." This ancient gateway lost its identity some years ago, being swallowed up by modern walls. To the left, standing alone, is seen a great chocolate colored tower capped by a quaint cone, seeming without either door or windows. This is the famous "camouflé" tower, afterward named for the brave bombardier honored in the chronicles of Metz as one of its defenders. It is now closed to visitors and deserted. I should have liked to explore it, but I could find no way to accomplish this.

The gate called Saint-Thiebault is of the eighteenth century. Here were the earliest walls of the town. It is said that there was a great amphitheater here in Roman times, and underneath are vast subterranean passages, some of which are unexplored, and that many fragments of columns and carved stones are there.

In 1445 was erected the ancient gray gateway called the "Porte des Allemands." It is a matter of history that this fortified château was constructed during the time of an assault and siege. A tablet inserted in the outer walls bears the name of the architect, Henri de Baconval, and the date of its completion. There are four great machicolated towers, and an interior cloister of unique character. It takes its name from the Teutonic cavaliers, the Hospitaliers of Our Lady. Farther on is the Porte Sainte Barbe, with an inscription in old French, "When we have bread inside, we have peace outside" (Quand nous avons pain dedans, nous avons paix de fors) [de hors]. Here and there about the old town are many picturesque and delightful corners, and on some of the quays are charming ancient façades, and most venerable walls, whose tall windows and delightful hanging balconies all decked with bright blossoms and vines are mirrored in the still waters below, where many weatherbeaten punts are tied to posts and rings in the mossy walls. On some of these balconies one may be the amused witness of the manner of the various household economies of the people, all carried on with delightful frankness. The old streets away from the busy centers which are so crowded with soldiers and bustle, are filled with charm and poetry. In some of these are old dark houses with high walls and doorways reached by breakneck stairways, and it is to be remarked that on these old tottering balconies, and in the grimiest of these windows, high and low, are invariably pots of brightest flowers.

An immense stone bridge of thirteen arches crosses the river Moselle. It is named curiously the Bridge of Skeletons (Pont-des-Morts), but there is nothing "macabresque" about its present appearance to justify its funereal name. It is said that in the thirteenth century there was a bridge here which was so old that it fell down. In order to build another the town authorities granted to the hospital, in return for a certain sum of money, the right to claim from each patient who died the best shirt or coat he owned. Verily there must have been either a tremendous mortality among the patients, or else their clothing must have been of incredible value. From this bridge there is a fine view of the Cathedral over the trees and the tiled roofs. At the bridge of Sailly, over the narrow stream one had formerly a view of the tanneries, an important industry of Metz. This picture has now disappeared, and in its place is a narrow street over the river, on each side of which are tall wooden houses all decked with open floors, as if their walls had tumbled outward, exposing dark, noisome interiors below, where were vast piles of hides in hideous bundles lying about, among which passed the dim figures of men naked to the waist in seemingly endless procession,—and the smells!—and again the *smells!!*

Metz has an interesting library containing some valuable books and various MSS. bearing upon the history of Alsace-Lorraine, and a museum, both in the Bibliothek Strasse. The museum has some Roman antiquities, and a sarcophagus in marble in which, so it is claimed, reposed the remains of Louis-le-Debonnaire in the Abbey of Saint Arnulphe. Adjoining the library in the Geisberg Strasse is the Austrasian Palace erected upon the site of an ancient Roman Palace in 1599. Some of the stones used in this building were those forming the outer walls of the earlier structure. The hand of the Teutonic "restorer" is seen in the "ornamentation" of this venerable building, now used as a commissariat depot for the German garrison.

North of the town is found the Chambiére Cemetery, in which is an impressive memorial monument erected to the French soldiers who perished at Metz in 1870. What one remembers chiefly about Metz is the vast number of soldiers thronging the streets and filling the restaurants, both humble and pretentious; the street cars and omnibuses, and the roads in and out of the town. It is estimated that one out of every three in the town population of seventy thousand is a soldier, but this may be an exaggeration. Nevertheless, fresh arrivals of regiments were reported while we were there. In the night one could hear the tramp, tramp of marching feet, and the rumbling of great vans following the troops. The French people with whom we talked regarded these military movements as ordinary occurrences; they were used to them, and they excited neither comment nor interest. I have heard a great deal about the ill manners of the soldiers, and the unbearable and intolerable insolence of the officers towards the civilian, and also almost unbelievable tales of their behaviour toward women.

I felt bound to investigate the matter for myself, so that in writing of them I should not do these men injustice. I watched and studied their actions, both on the street and in the restaurants and cafés which they frequented. These were the Kaiser-Pavillon on the Esplanade; the Rheinischer Hof, and the beer houses, Germania and the Burgerbrau, Kaiser-Wilhelm Platz. The officers were generally fine looking, well set up men, mustachioed like the Kaiser, and seemingly devoted to the "punctilio." They were jolly of manner and affable among themselves. But here it ended. To the shopmen and towards the civilian their manner was not civil. It was indeed haughty and intolerant to the last degree

—indeed, again—it was brusque and masterful. Attention to requests was not asked; it was demanded. If not instantly heeded there was trouble for the offender. But I saw no violence offered at any time, such as I was led to expect after reading of the Zabern affair.

Their attitude towards women was one of extreme gallantry, and, at least so far as I could see, this attitude was not at any time resented by the object of their attentions. I had been told that the officers walking two and three abreast on the pavement in the afternoon promenade, would never step aside to allow a lady to pass; indeed that they would on the contrary push her aside. I saw nothing of this, I am bound to say. It may have been true in individual cases, but it certainly was not their practice in the town of Metz as far as I was able to see. I gathered that the people fondly hoped . . . yes, they *hoped*, that one day—ah! blessed longed-for day!—that their beloved Alsace-Lorraine would be again in the bosom of the Mother Country. But meanwhile . . .

M. Emile Hinzelin, Director of "La France de Demain," says, "During the early days of the war, 1914–15, the Germans caused the great bell, the 'Mute,' in the Cathedral to ring without cessation in honor and celebration of their imaginary victories, but the thundering of the great guns of the approaching French put courage and hope in the hearts of the Messins. On the reverse of a photograph of the Place d'Arms of Metz, a correspondent wrote to a friend in Paris under date of November, 1914, 'We hear you, and we await you.'

"General Ferdinand Foch (pronounced Fosh), who was appointed Supreme Commander of the Allied Forces on March 29, 1918, while of Basque origin, born at Tarbee in 1851, was raised here at Metz. After the annexation of Lorraine, in 1871, rather than become a German subject he returned to France. Entering the Polytechnic School in Paris under the number 72, he was a rather slow pupil, leaving his class numbered forty-five, which did not offer any hopes of a great or brilliant future. He was noted as a conscientious student and a close applicant. His great passion was the study of strategy of war, particularly the war of 1870, in its most minute details. From his knowledge of the peculiar mentality of the Germans, he counted upon their repeating in future conflicts the manœuvres in which they had been so successful. He believed, too, that they would inevitably repeat their mistakes. In all his writings and teachings at the Superior War School, he held always to the idea of an inevitable aggression by Germany, sprung with lightning-like rapidity, after long premeditation and most minute preparation—the swift thunderbolt of the opening to develop into a struggle of colossal proportions. . . .

"Foch led the 7th French army at the Battle of the

Marne, and later the offensive between Armentieres and Arras in the spring of 1915. After these operations he was surpassed in public opinion of the French Army Chiefs by Generals Petain and Nivelle, whose wonderful leadership before Verdun made them famous. When General Petain succeeded Nivelle last May as Commander-in-Chief in the field, General Foch took his place as Chief of Staff in Paris." (N. Y. *Times*, Mar. 30, '18.) In the April following he was appointed chief of the Allied forces in France.

Strassburg

Strassburg

E were two among the thousand or more people who stood shoulder to shoulder in a contracted space not large enough to hold half that number with comfort. Overhead towered the great Cathedral, before us its immense pink-gray fabric, with statues dim of outline and detail, and a myriad of pinnacles and elaborate Gothic lacework. If we had awakened suddenly in this strange place, we should have marveled at the sight; as it was, we were rather phlegmatic, but certainly expectant. Our position in the square had been achieved somewhat laboriously, as had that of our neighbors who surrounded us. We had left our distant lodging place by taximeter cab (fifty pfennigs for each thousand yards, by the way) and slowly threaded narrow streets, and crossed bridges, and traversed quaint squares with names which we found difficult to pronounce properly or intelligibly to our square-headed driver, and had noted ancient house fronts and quaint gables marked for future inspection; to be all at once halted by a German policeman who resembled the effigies of Bismarck, and to be told by him with scant courtesy that our taxi could go no further; that we must get out and join the crowd on foot.

The streets were still damp with the rain, and the atmosphere was saturated with it. From the railway station we followed the crowd through the Kuhngasse to the canalized river Ill, through the Kleber-Staden, past the Romanesque Synagogue, and the old market, where there was some sort of an exhibition going on; crossed the Kronenburg Bridge, and by the Alte Weinmarkt, with its monumental fountain, we were pushed and hustled along with and by the crowd. Reaching the Weinmarkt Strasse we were somewhat more comfortable, for this wide street is one of the main arteries of traffic. In the Hohe-steg we saw the Eisern-Manns-Platz and the famous little iron figure on the house front, from which the Platz takes its name. Then we were again pushed and hustled along, past the bronze statue of Kleber, to the arcaded Gewerbslauben, leading through the Gutenberg Platz, past the statue of the inventor of the "art preservative of arts," and here we were at last in the Kramergasse before the west façade of the great Minster.

The crowd about us was formed of various social strata. Some of the men wore the red and green ribbon of an imperial order. One wore the red button of the Legion of Honor of France. I recognized the distinctive costumes of peasants from both "Haut" and "Bas" Alsace, both men and women. Some wore coarse costumes from the remote villages of the Black Forest. There seemed to be more women than men in the multitude. Some of them were handsome, others showed in their faces the brutalizing effect of their servile existence.

We noted that there was a great deal of French spoken by the people about us, much more than German. Near us was a tall Frenchwoman of great volubility. With her was a very stout, short Alsatian lady wearing the distinctive headdress of wide black ribbon. The first discussed with her companion her plans of seeing all that was possible, in tones audible to all about her.

"Rosalie," she said, "I shall with great skill make the push, and then you should immediately follow me. Thus, shall I do it."

As she spoke, she illustrated the movement she intended to make, by means of a large thick blue umbrella which she carried. It struck squarely in the back of a very stout woman in front, who turned about with a face so flaming with wrath that the offender was forced to apologize.

"I ask pardon, Madame," said the tactician, "I saw you not."

"Then, Madame," returned the stout lady in icy tones, "you must indeed be blind."

"I have asked pardon, Madame," said the offender, indignantly pursing up her lips. "It was an accident that can happen, and one to be overlooked at once, and with the amiability customary among people who are used to good society, more especially as the crowd is great, and one was pushed from behind, Madame."

"Your pardon, Madame," returned the stout one, with voice growing husky from rage, "but I overheard you planning your 'push' with your friend."

"But of a certain, Madame," flung back the other, shaking the fat blue umbrella in her face, "my conversation was intended for the ears of the lady who accompanies me. One in good society does not listen to and repeat conversation not addressed to one."

"Evidently, Madame," spurted the other vehemently; "but Madame must remember that the voices of uncultivated persons are both loud and penetrating. The voice of a lady, Madame, is rarely either loud or penetrating, Madame," and she appealed to all about her for confirmation, and there were both nods and shakes of the head in return. Clearly the sentiment of the crowd about us was with the last speaker.

"I shall withdraw myself from the proximity of a person whom I hold so objectionable, Madame," hurled back the aggressive one in a fury.

"Perfectly, Madame; do that quickly, Madame, I beseech you," smiled sweetly the injured one, "and with the quickness extraordinary."

The aggressive lady pushed and squirmed her way into a new place well to the left, but still within hearing.

Unhappily for her in some way her fidgeting about brought the blue umbrella in contact with the small of the back of a tall, red faced, grizzled and military looking gentleman, who at once jumped aside as well as he could in the crowd and turned ferociously upon her. Fresh and equally elaborate apology was entered upon, and then ensued the following dialogue:

"Mille pardon, M'sieur. An accident, I assure you."

"It is less than nothing, Madame. I pray you do not speak of it."

"Some one behind pushed me, dear sir."

"It was nothing, Madame; I did not even notice it. 'Twas less than nothing, I repeat. Perhaps I crowded Madame."

"Not at all, Monsieur, but I fear that I may 'derange' Monsieur again, and then I should be 'desolé.' If I could be permitted to take that little place before Monsieur, not *directly* before Monsieur, you understand, but just a little to one side, so that I should not incommode Monsieur, that would infinitely oblige me and render me in debt to Monsieur a thousand fold."

The military person yielded his place and elevated his eyebrows at the same moment. "Au gr-r-rande plaisir, Madame," he shot at her, while he caressed the sore spot in the small of his back. There were knowing smiles exchanged by those about who had followed the incident. She had gained her point, and also had succeeded in drawing with her the friend, who heaved her way through the packed throng bestowing "pardons" and "mille fois" impartially, and carrying through it all a sweet smile of innocent good humor that remained on her face in spite of all the scowls and remonstrances of those she pushed aside. We could not but admire the way in which it was accomplished.

All this bustle and stir, and the eager expectancy of the crowd was most entertaining and amusing to us, albeit the Lady Anne abhors crowds, because she cannot see what is going on, unless by happy chance I am able to find some elevated point of vantage where she can comfortably see over the heads of the throng without being pushed and jostled.

This I found in the window over a bake shop, where, for the expenditure of a silver piece to the domestic and the announcement of our nationality, the portly wife of the baker made us welcome, and gave us comfortable chairs at the lace hung open window of her "salon," where we sat for an hour or more eating delicious fresh small cakes for which our hostess would accept no pay, and watching the crowd in the street and the square beyond, while she entertained us with such information as travelers seek in a strange city. It was some great church feast that we were witnessing, and such events always bring forth the bourgeoisie, which lives most frugally, and having seemingly abundant leisure, is ever greedy to be present and take part in any street spectacle or ceremony.

There were stalwart helmeted troopers of the cavalry or the City Guard, and constantly their shrill trumpet calls rang out nearby and were answered from afar. The crowd beneath the window good naturedly made way for a small two-wheeled green cart, driven by a red-cheeked woman and laden with brightly polished milk cans. The cart was drawn by a diminutive donkey in a brass studded harness, with a large bright red worsted tassel under each long, restless ear. The police stopped its further progress, and there it remained. The red-cheeked woman took out from under the seat a huge half loaf of rye bread, from which she cut a slice for herself and one for the donkey, and both ate contentedly. Now came a band of children laden with baskets, strewing the open way with leaves, flowers, and bright colored paper fragments, under which the pavement well nigh disappeared in a charming mosaic of red, green and white. Heavy church bells boomed out melodiously, and were answered by joyous and sweeter peals from others in the distance.

Then all at once came the clang of brass cymbals, and the blare of horns, mingled with the rich harmony of chanting voices, as the banners of the procession came into view. We were struck with the number of young girls there were in the procession, so many of whom were in white, wearing long veils thrown back; all young and pretty; of all ages, from the tiny tot in stiff starched dress to the tall, lithe maid who bore the heavy white gold emblazoned banner of the Virgin; on they came with quick step, and passed out of sight through the sombre clad crowd—whole squadrons of them in white, or lilac, or pink, each led by a maiden who bore the banner, or emblem, or reliquary or even in one instance a heavy oaken crucifix. Sometimes there came a group of sacred effigies on platforms upborne by six or a dozen girls, and to these were attached lines of bright ribbons, the ends of which were held by young girls who walked alongside. On streamed the procession, demurely marching to the strains of the mellow bassoon, the curiously shaped serpent cornet, the cylindrical red and black striped drum of archaic shape, and clashing cymbal upon which the players, perchance gathered from many a distant village, piped and beat their very best in honor of the Saint, whoever he was.

At times all this noise ceased as if by magic, and the mellow, deep voices of the chanting priests broke soothingly upon the ear, followed by the clear, tender voices of children, as school after school, and all admirably drilled and officered by shaven priests and placid-faced nuns, passed below us. We marvelled at the well thought out theatrical effect of color, and the skill with which the ecclesiastical treasures were displayed to the people. We reflected, too, with humility upon certain tawdrinesses of detail in our own celebrations in the land of the free, for which we tried to find valid excuses.

Here was a marvel of color and grouping. Where could we secure such old lace as adorned the robes of the ecclesiastics who walked past our window beneath canopies of scarlet velvet embroidered with real gold cord? An Empress might covet it without hope. Drawn for the occasion from the old carved chest in the treasury of the Cathedral, where it lies safely wrapped, it was the pious labor of fair, slender fingers that had crumbled away to dust nearly three centuries ago. And that heavy casket of repoussé gold studded with jewels "en cabochon," borne by the four shaven priests, which the baker's wife told us contained the wonder working relic, the finger of the Saint; where in our country could we see such master goldsmith work, such a triumph of art and skill? Madame asked us if we had such in New York? And I answered the question as truthfully as I could, admitting much yet, I think, maintaining our civic pride, as I was bound to do. But Lady Anne was not content with what she considered my inadequate defence, and marshalled an astonishing array of facts to prove that our well known appreciation of art was indeed art preservative, which eloquence quite overcame our hostess.

Onward below us swept the seemingly endless procession—as if the whole feminine population of the province between the ages of seven and twenty had been summoned into the service. Then new phalanxes of chanting priests, some strangely clad; of deep voiced prelates of grave, solemn mien, whose orange or scarlet cloaks seemed frosted with the costly lace, and whose melodious voices rang out in the quaint street. Lumbering carts all hung with rare tapestries and containing stiffly swaying waxen effigies of sacred personages and large brass crucifixes passed by. Others resplendent with candelabra and altar cloths of priceless fabric interwoven with golden threads flashed in the sunlight. And still the childish treble of the young choristers, intermingled with the deep diapason of the priestly chant, rolled on.

Lady Anne exclaimed aloud as the prettiest of the sights came into view—a tiny child—a boy with beautiful face and golden curls, clad in a fur robe, carrying a small, slender cross, and leading a snow white lamb, which followed him most docilely—a charming model of innocence such as one sees in the wonderful paintings of the Italian masters—this representative of the youthful John the Baptist, with filleted head, and slender bare limbs, marched along, seemingly all unconscious of the impression he made.

We noted that the people were variously impressed;

some seemed coldly indifferent and failed to salute as the holy emblems passed. Others, and these we recognized as the lower orders of peasants, knelt in humbleness and bared their heads. Between these extremes were the "bourgeoisie," so called, who seemed impressed by the solemnity, but who maintained a critical attitude. But we were quite satisfied by the milk woman of the rosy countenance, who knelt on the seat of the small green cart among the polished brass cans, fingering her rosary with its large brown beads and brass medallions, "telling" them as devoutly as one could wish.

There must be much rivalry between the different parishes as to the display, and the various musical companies and their bands. These jealously guarded emblems and canopies from far off chapel sacristies and chancels so venerated and brought out so rarely into the sunlight. These pilgrims from the famous old shrines of the Rhine must endeavor not to be outdone or outshone by the metropolitans. Saint Ursula of the network of dark, ancient streets, where medieval houses rear their picturesque gables, now tenanted by the lowly poor, must make proper showing before the parvenu districts, where new stucco and shining glass shelter the rich.

And all at once the tumult of cymbal and loud horn was hushed, and only the rich diapason of the chanting was heard. The crowd below surged forward and stood on tiptoe the better to see. Plainly something was to happen—perhaps the chief event of the celebration. Then it came;—surrounded by a cohort of chanting priests most sombrely clad in dark robes as if to lend effect by contrast, and preceded by scarlet and white clad acolytes swinging smoke censers all beneath a large silken state "baldaquin" or canopy, borne by eight men, came a figure who wore no mitre, but who was resplendent in jewels, gold embroidered cloak, and collar of ancient lacework. He walked slowly and majestically —an old, thin-faced man, with silvery white hair, chanting in a high-pitched, reedy voice. . . . He passed from our sight, tottering beneath the magnificent "baldaquin" amidst clouds of blue incense. The crowd surged in behind him, and soon the street below was empty. The milk woman gathered up the reins and whacked them on the donkey's back; away went the little green cart, the brass cans rattling loudly. The procession was out of sight. The great spectacle for which we had come to Strassburg was over.

Fainter grow the sounds of the music and the chanting of the priests. The sunlight had departed and the shadows were beginning to gather. Across the street in a doorway we could see the figure of a brown clad friar standing as if in a trance. His hands grasped a rosary and it seemed as if he were praying, though he was too far away for his face to be clearly seen. He seemed to us then like a statue of some hermit saint carved in the gloom of the old doorway—but while we watched the door opened and he passed into its shadow out of our ken.

At the "table d'hôte," we fell into conversation with a most affable and good humored individual, of great volubility, who proved to be a retired Captain of Artillery of the French Army of 1871, and a native of Strassburg, who gave us among other valuable information a well written account of the origin of the "Marseillaise" or, as he in common with all Strassburgers insisted upon calling it, the "Strassbourgeoise," which is as follows: On the 20th of April, 1792, France declared war upon Austria. Five days later the Mayor of Strassburg, Dietrich, with the men of the regiments of the Garrison, and detachments of the National Guard, placarded the principal streets with the declaration of war, in both French and German. At each posting of the placard the band played the song of the epoch, "Ca Ira." On his return to his home, No. 4 Place de Broglie, the Mayor received, among other friends, a young Captain, from Lons-le-Saulnier, named Rouget de l'Isle, aged thirty-two years. Dietrich addressed his colleagues as follows: "We have entered upon the campaign, and we need another sort of song to inspire our soldiers. The municipality of Strassburg opens a concourse, offering a prize for the best composition."

Young de l'Isle returned to his quarters in the Caserne, was seized with an inspiration, and there and then com-

posed a song of both words and music, which he played
over and over again, cutting and pruning far into the
night, and in the morning at seven o'clock he called in a
brother officer named Maslet, or Masclet, to whom he
sang it, to the latter's great enthusiasm.   In the evening
there was a gathering of patriots at the house of Mayor
Dietrich, and it was there that Rouget de Lisle, accompanied upon the piano by Dietrich's niece, sang the song
known the world over to-day by the name of the "Marseillaise."

One of the company arranged for its publication in
Strassburg under the title of "Chant de guerre pour
l'armée du Rhyn, dedié au Maréchal Luckner, Com-
mandant en Chef de l'armée."   On the 29th of April following, it was played in the Place du Broglie in Strassburg by the band of the 1st Battalion of the Rhine-Loire
Volunteers, and received instant popularity, moving the
assembled people to great enthusiasm.   Played in Mar-
seilles in July of the same year, it was unanimously
adopted by the army of volunteers, its ringing refrain
sung by the troops entering Paris in the month of August,
moving the populace almost to tears.   The Parisians
named it "The Marseillaise," in spite of its published
title, and so it has remained.   But it is really the
"Strassbourgeoise," and is invariably thus named
throughout Alsace-Lorraine.   The song at first had but
six stanzas of ten lines each, and, according to the best

authorities, the seventh, attributed to the poet Marie Joseph Chenier, is really the composition of a priest of Vienne (Isere). It runs as follows:

> "Nous entrerons dans la carrière
> Quand nos aines n'y seront plus;
> Nous y trouverons leur poussière
> Et la trace de leurs vertus. (bis)
> Bien moins jaloux de leur survivre
> Que de partager leur cercueil,
>   Nous aurons le sublime orgueil
> De les venger ou de les suivre.
> Aux armes, citoyens! Formez vos battaillons
> Marchons! (bis). Qu'un sang abreuve nos sillons!"

The eyes of the old Alsatian blazed as he recited these words in our little salon that rainy afternoon. We were glad that we invited him to have his coffee with us after dinner, for when he found that we were eager listeners, and that he could trust us, he unbosomed himself of his pent-up feelings. He was an interesting talker, but we gathered no facts from his conversation which we had not already heard in other towns, and which are not already set down in the opening chapters of this chronicle. But what he told us of the "Strassbourgeoise" was most interesting.

"La Marseillaise" was thus named by decree of the 28th Messidor of the year III. "Hymn àpart, fougueux, enlevant, irresistible, empreint a la fois de joie et de tristesse, de colère et de passion, un chant civique sorti des flancs du peuple et de son fier courroux contre l'étranger et l'envahisseur." [1] It is now forbidden to sing this song in Alsace-Lorraine. It is forbidden by the German law even to have a copy of the song in one's possession. What a strange destiny was his who composed this great song; and his to whom it was dedicated, the savant Frederic de Dietrich. The brave Marshal Luckner was decapitated by the Jacobins, and the poet himself incarcerated under the terror, because the hymn was considered a song of protest and violence against the French! . . .

The old city of Strassburg is so remarkable that one cannot resist giving here a short historical sketch which may be skipped if the reader is so minded. It was at the end of the Roman epoch that a Bishopric was created in the city "Argentoratum," and the faithful built a church in which to celebrate their cult. During the "Frank" period the Cathedral was already situated on the present site of the Minster and dedicated to the Holy Virgin Mary, and at the right of the principal altar was one consecrated to Saint Paul and another to Saint Peter. This church was pillaged and burned in April, 1002, by the soldiers of Herman, Duke of Suabia. Later the ruins were entirely destroyed by lightning and no trace remained. Bishop Wernher soon commenced the construction of a new church, employing thousands of masons and

[1] Henri Welschinger.

peasant laborers, who brought from the quarries of Wasselone and Marlenheim the great blocks of stone from the Vosges, which give to the Cathedral its beautiful rosy tint. After it was completed, it was burned and ruined during the years 1130, 1140, 1150 and 1176. However, it was not entirely destroyed, for a part of the original choir is still pointed out in the crypt. Soon after the latter date, Bishop Conrad I began the reconstruction, promising to the faithful certain indulgences in return for their donations. So on the 7th of September, 1275, according to the chronicle, on the day of the fête of the Nativity of the Virgin, under the reign of Rodolph of Hapsbourg, the tower was dedicated. Of this nothing remains save the portal and the towers.

The Cathedral thus developed from the east to the west, and the choir is the most ancient part, resting upon the crypt, which was constructed by Wernher. The transept, forming the small arms of the cross, was erected during this epoch, and presents traces of Roman and Gothic. The portal on the place "de l'Évêché" is entirely Roman. Here are the two admirable statues of the Old and New Testament, with the cross and the chalice. The celebrated pillar of the Angels with the trumpets; the figure of Christ and three Angels carrying instruments of the Passion, are pure Gothic. The nave was constructed in 1250-75, and is entirely French Gothic, by French architects, and presents the grandest analogy with that of the church of Saint Denis. German architects had little or nothing to do with it. The eminent architect, Ralph Adams Cram, in his scholarly work, "Heart of Europe," (p. 294) says: "It is at Strassburg that we find that singular and ingenious masterpiece, the 'Pillar of the Angels,' slender grouped shafts with intermediate niches, one above the other, each containing an exquisite statue of an apostle, an angel, or, at the top, our Lord at the Day of Judgment. This is one of those sudden and unprecedented happenings in medieval art that mark the vast vitality, imagination, and personal initiative of the time."

The master work of the Cathedral is due to one man, whose name is mentioned for the first time in the chronicle as Master Erwin, but whose birthplace is doubtful. It was he who designed the occidental face of the Cathedal, with its three wonderful portals, its incomparable rose window, and its statues and innumerable statuettes. In the tympanum of the great doorway is a series of sculptures representing the whole history of the Old Testament from the Creation to Jonah and the whale. For the most part the great statues are ancient, but the smaller ones are those restored or imitated to replace those destroyed during the Revolution.

The Cathedral has always excited general admiration. In 1481, the Duke Jean Galeas Sforza wrote to the Council of Strassburg, asking for the name of an architect

capable of directing the construction of the great Dome
of Milan. The Council unanimously agreed upon
Jacques de Landschut. He it was who designed and
superintended the construction of the exquisite portal of
Saint Laurent (see drawing). The town of Strassburg
being converted to Protestantism in 1559 High Mass
was not again celebrated in the Cathedral until 1681,
when Louis XIV restored it to the Catholics. In 1772–78
the architect Jean-Laurent Goetz enclosed the monument
on the north and south sides by a beautiful arcade in
pure Gothic style. The Cathedral suffered much from
the bombardment during the Franco-Prussian war.
After peace was declared the "flèche," which leaned over
dangerously, threatening to fall, was repaired, but it was
not until 1878 that the beautiful "tourelle" and the transept were completed! [1]

The interesting and voluble retired Captain of Artillery proved to be a veritable mine of information, and
was most amiable in his responses to our many questions.
"And now," said he, "you have visited our noble and
beautiful Cathedral, do you not, Monsieur and Gracious
Lady, find your sensations to be all enthusiastic? Our
noble Cathedral, which, by its magnificent façade, its
'rosaces,' its statues and statuettes, its thousands of
motifs drawn from the flora of Alsace; its grand nave,

[1] See "La Cathedral de Strasbourg." Georges Delahache, Paris, Longuet
Edit.

and the great clock, the only one of its kind in all the world, have you not content with it all? Have you found in other Cathedrals such magnificent high reliefs? —such graceful columns?—And the windows! Where else will you find such delicious melting tones of purple, gold and azure?—Our noble Cathedral is really an object of veneration, of an intense and unalterable affection, so associated is it with our history, that one cannot speak or write of Alsace without allusion to it. It is really the heart of Strassburg. To know it properly one must ascend to the platform of the tower, and there become familiar with the choir, and the towers of the 'abside.' And once upon the platform of the great tower—"

Here his enthusiasm rendered him speechless—his eyes raised comically to the ceiling, one hand upon his breast, covering the medal or decoration which he wore, the other raised to his lips with thumb and finger tips together.

"The view incomparable," he at length continued with a sigh of rapture. "Over the rosy red tiled roofs of our noble city, the eye travels to the distant, dim Vosges, with its cluster of ancient châteaux, the noble Mount Sainte-Odile; the great Hohenkoenigsbourg and the rim of the Black Forest. We can there contemplate the beautiful plains of Alsace, with its picturesque valleys, its golden hillsides and misty hills. Was not the great Goethe justified, Monsieur and Gracious Lady, when he described our Province as 'a new Paradise prepared for the human race.' These were the words of the poet written when he was a student here at the University. See, too, how capriciously the picturesque streets stretch away in all directions under our eyes, like unto the filaments of a gigantic web. One must really see a sunset from the tower, and I hope that Monsieur and Madame will not fail to do so before they leave Strassburg. The rays of the sun there remind me of the days when I was a child, when I was taken to see the fire-works which were set off in the tower on the great fête days. Those white and red flames pouring out from the lace work of the old tower, white and red; the colors of our ancient Alsatian banner, I shall never forget them! . . ."

Tears came to his eyes, and he brushed them away without shame. "Monsieur and Madame saw yesterday our great fête of the 'Assumption.' Was it not a superb procession? It was in memory of the vow of Louis XIII. You saw the sacred Image of the Virgin with outstretched arms bearing the Infant Jesus. You saw, too, the great silken banners of the town of Strassburg borne on either hand. In the days of 'Louis le Debonnaire' the seal of Strassburg bore the image of the Virgin Mother with the legend 'Virgo, roga prolem quo cives servet et urbem.' There was carried formerly a great gold embroidered banner, which was destroyed in the bombardment of 1870. Upon this was shown the figure of the Infant Jesus holding a 'fleur de lys' in his hand. And according to record the ancient banners of the town all bore the 'fleur de lys' as part of the arms."

And certainly we did revel in the mild delights of the old Cathedral, approached by tortuous streets between amorphous houses of steep roofs, with many windows and dormers, and aged, carven doors surmounted at times by strange old trade emblems; their stories sometimes over-hanging in most satisfying manner. There were, too, rough cobbled market places with odd buildings, on which were pepperbox turrets, arcades and occasionally forgotten and weatherbeaten statued Saints, where good wives chaffered their wares on rainy market days. Here clings the soul of antiquity. We found a sort of Ark; a Saints' Sarcophagus, with a strange moss-grown recum-bent figure under the stone altar. Likewise an old triple fountain gushing from its grotto by the side of the street, called, so a shopkeeper told us, Saint Willibrod's Well, which, he said, was older than any record, and informed us that masons would come that very day to tear it away to build a new shop front. There was, too, a quaint and unspoiled age-worn haven, the little Hospice of Irmine, where lived twelve poor old men. "They might," said the shopkeeper, in answer to our question, "show it, but 'tis not the custom." But the Superieure, a gentle little old lady, in response to a pull at the bell handle, does us the honors of the quaint little row of buildings along the narrow court yard, the sacrosanct, the tiny chapel, the few happy dotards dozing in the sunlight. . . .

Up the dim pilgrim-worn staircase of the Cathedral to the platform, whatever curious beauty is in old gables, whatever charm there is in studying them, is here to be found. Closely all around they press, these oldest of gables all unchanged, as though they loved the protecting presence of the Cathedral. Teufelsdroch has described the joys he found in tiles. Here you may sit at the heart of Strassburg and be drawn into the beat of its old simple life. If you have anything of this love of quaint roofs, here you may revel in them.

The date of the completion of the first Minster is unknown. While the apse and the transept were slowly progressing, Gothic architecture had become established in France, and exercised everywhere its influence upon such constructions. The office of Cathedral architect is said to have long remained in the family after Erwin's death in 1348. The last practitioner is supposed to be a Master Gerlach. It was he who, in 1365, completed the third stage of the towers. Evidently the original plans were mislaid thereafter, because a platform, not the work of Erwin, was constructed between the towers. One Ulrich von Elsingen of Suabia then took up the work in 1399. This man showed an astonishing knowledge of design and command of construction work. He heightened the octagonal structure of the tower by adding another story, and thus it remained. The open-work spire is said not to be the work of Erwin. It is by all accounts the work of one Johann Hultz, who came from Cologne.

The work of the following centuries is easily traced if one is interested. The bombardment by the Germans in 1870 resulted in much damage, but all trace of this has disappeared under the "careful" restoration by an architect named Klotz. A new copper roof has been completed, and a curious sort of Romanesque dome constructed over the crossing. Some of this work of restoration has been under the superintendence of one Fr. Smitz, who was "Minster Architect," completing the great Cathedral at Cologne.

Of these old roofs and gables I made many sketches, and showing these one day in the hotel, I overheard two Frenchmen discussing us, and airing the while much Gallic wit at our expense, all harmless enough, too, be it said. "Mais v'la," I heard, "que M'sieur est tout-à-fait Americain! Qu'il est pratique, propre aux affaires! M'sieur voudrait bien, sans doute, acheter ces toits et l'emporter 'vec lui a New York! Que de justesse; comme c'est caracteristique!" etc.—and then "M'sieu will, in all probability, buy the great clock to take over to America!" This is, with the people, the great "pièce de resistance." It bears the inscription: "Voilà l'horloge astronomique a mouvement perpetuel."

STRASSBURG

This clock is not the original one, however. The first one was constructed in 1352; a second at the end of the sixteenth century, which was destroyed during the revolution. The present machine was made by the clockmaker Schwilgne, who died in 1856. Only a few parts of the framework, a wheel or two and some of the decorative paintings of the old clock by Dasypodius were used in the present clock. Each day at noon a crowd of tourists and curious ones gather before the ornamental railing before it, to await the loud crowing of the cock upon the summit of the structure. Upon the first gallery an angel strikes the quarters on a bell held in his hand; while a figure at his side reverses a sand glass on the hour. Above appears a skeleton, and around him are grouped figures supposed to represent childhood, youth, manhood, and old age. Beneath the first balcony the Saint proper to that day steps out of a niche when the hour strikes. A complete planetarium, behind which is a perpetual calendar, is set in motion by the mechanism, which, by some mysterious cunning, is made to regulate itself and adapt its motions to the revolution of the seasons for an apparently unlimited space of time.

Much cannot be said for the construction and architectural design of the clock. It might have been made a great work of art; worthy of the great and prominent place it occupies in the Cathedral, instead of which it is most clumsy and heavy in design. Only the top is

Gothic in form; all the rest is hopelessly German, and as bizarre as only a German could make it. In fine, it is only to be regarded as an ugly, big, and remarkably accurate clock.

In Strassburg whatever remains of the artistic and picturesque is clearly of French origin. Wherever the Germans have erected a building there is seen clumsiness, misapplication and misunderstanding of the principles of art. "That singular and ingenious masterpiece," as Mr. Ralph Adams Cram has called it, "the Pillar of the Angels, with its exquisitely slender and graceful clustered shafts interrupted with canopied niches containing each a wonderfully sculptured Angel or Apostle, is all French Gothic in its purest form, owing nothing to German skill. Such works of art spring into being miraculously, marking the necessity of expression of the moment. It is born of deep feeling and enthusiasm. This shaft, which remains to us in all its purity, despite the German craze for reconstruction, is the work of Erwin de Steinbach, a native of Strassburg, who was also the Master Architect of the Cathedral. In the House of our Lady (Frauenhause) is shown a statue of Erwin, who at his death left his favorite horse, and an annuity for the benefit of his beloved Cathedral. The epitaph to Erwin de Steinbach is chiseled in a stone in the chapel of Saint John the Baptist, and furnishes the date of his death as 1318, "Le Seize des Calendes de Fevrier." Above the central door of the façade, one may read this inscription: "Anno Domini 1277, in die beati urbani hoc gloriosum opus inchoavit Magister Erwinus de Steinbach."

In the House of Our Lady, in the Schlossplatz, which was built in the fourteenth century, is the ancient and most interesting plan of the Cathedral on sheets of parchment, together with a detailed drawing of the spire and the façade, and also the remains of the old clock. Mr. Cram pronounces the Strassburg Cathedral "much more interesting and poetic" than Cologne, "with greater refinement and originality in design, though its taste is far from impeccable, its structural sense gravely deficient. The tendency is wholly toward lace-like and fantastic design, but it has little resemblance to the late French flamboyant with its curving and intersticing lines; instead, it is more suggestive of the English perpendicular, with its scaffolding of vertical lines applied to, but not a part of, the basic fabric. It has no consistency of plan, for the eastern end, with its semicircular apse and portions of its transepts, is of a singularly noble type of the twelfth century Romanesque, while the nave is of the thirteenth century, and the tower and upper portion of the west front are a hundred years later.

"Confused as it is, there is an extraordinary charm about it all, for every part is personal and distinguished, full of novel and poetic ideas and all kinds of unaffected touches of genius. The wonderful color of the exterior and the singularly fine glass of the interior have much to do with its general effect of a delicate medieval loveliness that makes amends for its architectural shortcomings." [1]

Near the House of Our Lady is the ancient Palace of the Bishops of Strassburg, built by Cardinal Armand Gaston de Rohan in 1728, in which was held a most brilliant and notable court by the other three Bishops of the Rohan family. During the first Revolution it was used as town headquarters, and afterwards up to within a few years was part of the University. Lately it has been the Art Museum, for which purpose it is well fitted, having some magnificently decorated halls and rooms of the eighteenth century period. The majestic portal on the Cathedral Square gives access to the Court of Honor, where are some thirteenth century sarcophagi. The façade on the Ill is most sumptuous. I remember there a remarkable collection of little soldiers in metal representing the Grande Armée, the work of a citizen of the town, who must have spent years in making them. And a group of Prussian officers in uniform were studying them, pointing out to one another the miniature figure of the Great Napoleon, surrounded by his officers, before whom were arranged the long lines of grenadiers, dragoons and cuirassiers, as if in review.

Near the Cathedral also is the celebrated house called the Kammerzell, perhaps the most picturesque of all the

[1] "Heart of Europe." Ralph Adams Cram.

houses in Strassburg, of astonishing richness of design and carving and in a splendid state of preservation. It has three stories in relief, beautiful windows framed with curious sculptures, a façade of old oaken beams highly ornamented with the signs of the Zodiac, and a high, steep, pent roof pierced with three rows of small windows in antique fashion.

Following the rue du Dome (I use the French names by preference, rather than the uncouth German ones) one arrives at the Place de Broglie. Formerly this was the favorite promenade of the Strassburgers. Here one finds rows of cafés, which are well occupied by the people during the afternoon hours, gossiping and drinking the excellent beer on tap. A good military band plays here twice a week. Formerly the great yearly horse fair was held in this square, which the Romans named "Vetus Forum Equorum." Here, too, the Knights' Tourneys took place before the Dukes and their ladies. Opposite is the superb hotel of the "Intendance" of the eighteenth century, restored after the Franco-Prussian war.

Farther along the Ill, beyond the new Palace, is the ancient church of Saint-Pierre-le-Jeune, a splendid Gothic monument which lately has been ruined by a German architect in his villainous so-called "restorations," and his following of the German mania for painting chromatically everything in sight.

All over the town one sees evidence of this sort of German taste, in the University; the Postes and Telegraphes; the Banks, and the large heavily ornamented shop fronts. One flees from these horrors, and seeks the winding banks of the river Ill, bordered by pretty walled spaces, and quaint turrets, especially the old houses on the quai Saint-Jean; the quai Türckenheim, and the altogether charming quarter called "la petite France," inhabited by fishermen, with the three old square towers. Here are three old bridges, formerly fortified, of delightful character. There are ancient timbered houses on the neighboring quais of Saint-Nicholas and Des Pecheurs, with graceful "encorbellements," and noble lines. The antiquary finds here a mine of wealth in sculptured emblems, oriels, delicately balanced balconies railed with wrought iron, quaint galleries of carved wood, bearing strange effigies of armored knights and heads of bears and lions, with fabulous dragons winding about the pillars.

In the rue Serruriers is the old church of Saint Thomas, built upon the foundations of the ancient Palace of the Franks, which, history says, was "burnt in the year 1007," and as if this were not far enough back, mentions a previous convent which was here in 890. This old church is flanked by a great square tower, which is worth seeing, but the church is remarkable for the admirable monument or tomb of Marshal de Saxe, a magnificent mausoleum in marble, the chef-d'œuvre of Pigalls, over which he labored for seventeen years. It bears the inscription:

STRASSBURG

"Mauritio Saxoni, Curlandiæ et Semigalle
Ducisummo Regiorum Exercituum
Præfecto Semper Victori
LUDOVICS XV
Victoriarum anctor et
ipse Dux Poni Jussit. Obit
XXX Nov Ad: MDCCL Elatis LV,"

in precious homage to the illustrious victor of Fontenoy, dead in 1750 in the service of France. I know of no other tomb of such dignity or so fine as this throughout the region. The five figures are exquisitely wrought in detail, showing the Marshal descending bravely the steps leading to the tomb at the summons of Death, heedless of the outstretched hand of France, who seeks to restrain him. Power, with the attributes of Hercules, mourns his premature end, and there are symbolical animals grouped about artistically, such as the Leopard of England; the Lion of Holland and the Eagle of Austria, which last is represented falling backwards at the Marshal's side, symbolizing the three powers defeated by him in the Flemish wars.

The Place Saint Thomas brings us to the statue of Gutenberg, the work of David d'Angers, erected in 1840, four hundred years after the discovery of printing, and bearing the motto: "Et la Lumière fut." Gutenberg, it seems, lived here in Strassburg until 1444, when he went to Mayence to associate himself with Jean Fust and Pierre Scheffer. Owing to a dispute with these men he separated from them and established a printery for himself. Always in trouble, in debt, and ever improvident, he died in 1467, a pauper. The chronicle of the town describes him as follows: In the year 1434 there resided at Strassburg a young man, born at Mayence in 1400, named Johann Gensfleisch. As his family possessed a small property called "Zum Guten Berg" (The Good Mountain) "he also often called himself Gutenberg."

Near at hand is the site of the fine Library, where during the bombardment by the Germans in 1871 that incomparable collection of precious and rare volumes, painted glass, and, above all, the priceless illuminated manuscript of Herrade de Landsberg, the "Hortus Deliciarum," chef-d'œuvre of the Master, and known to savants the world over, was entirely destroyed. Of this masterpiece, M. Henri Welschinger (member de l'Institut), writes: "Marius Vachon (in 1882) has made an inventory of the lost treasures, and recalls mournfully that it was the Germany of Goethe, Kant and Schiller which burnt and destroyed it." Thanks to the erudition and patience of a French critic there remains to us the only important document saved from the debris of the Municipal Library of Strassburg, which was burnt by order of General Werder, who was called "the murderer" by the hapless people of the town.

The celebrated manuscript of Herrade de Landsberg, known the world over, was a sort of resumé of both profane and sacred history of the world from the Creation. According to the researches and discoveries of the Canon of Straub, and carried on by his successor Canon Keller (1879–99) under the authority and auspices of the Society for the Preservation of Alsatian Historical Monuments, Herrade de Landsberg was Abbess of the Monastery of Hohenburg, who had succeeded the Abbess Relinde, parent of Frederic Barberousse, Duke of Alsace and Suabia, and wrote and painted in 1180 the "Hortus Deliciarum," of which the original text was upon three hundred and forty-two sheets of vellum. Mentioned in the chronicle of Hohenbourg as being part of the castle's treasure in the year 1521, it afterwards passed into the hands of the Bishop Erasmus of Limbourg and Saverne, who retained it until 1609, when it was deposited at the Chartreuse of Molsheim, where it was copied by the monkish illuminators. In 1790 it was returned to the Library of the department, from which Canon Rumpler reclaimed it in 1794 in the name of the Landsberg family. Later the Library again regained possession of it through the efforts of the Director. Louis Philippe granted the Count de Bastard permission to make a copy of the wonderful manuscript and its illuminations for his work, "Peinture et ornement des manuscrits," on condition of furnishing a copy to the National Library. The Society of Alsace, profoundly moved by the loss of the original, ordered the publication, using the work of Count de Bastard and such fragments of reproductions found in the (Frauenhaus) House of Our Lady, and such sketches of Engelhard and others as they could find. The work is, of course, incomplete and more or less fragmentary, for out of a total of the three hundred and six original designs, only two hundred and thirty-two could be found, but even so it remains a magnificent monument to the skill of Herrade de Landsberg, one of the most remarkable personages of the Middle Ages, and one of the greatest glories of Alsace.

This pious Lady not only produced in the "Hortus Deliciarum" a collection of the poetry of the time, but arranged a sort of encyclopedia of the Sciences. The manuscript was written in German characters in the Latin of the twelfth century. On every page was a delicate painting illustrating the text. She made with the greatest care extracts of the Old and the New Testament, and the works of Saints Augustin, Isadore, Gregory, Jerome, Saint John Chrysostome, Pierre Lombard, Bede, Clement Romain, etc., denoting great and extended erudition upon her part. Dissertations upon chronology, astronomy, geography, mythology were contained in the work entitled "Aurea Gemma." It contained a sort of "cantique" or "salut," addressed by the author to her companions at the monastery of Hohenbourg. The exact text is as follows: "Rhymthmus Herradis abbatissal per quam Hohenburgensis Virgunculas amabiliter salutat et veri Sponsi fidem dilectionemque salubriter invitat." After a "cantique" of Invocation, Herrade wrote a preface in Latin prose explaining the purpose of her books, saying that it was called the Jardin des Dèlices because it was composed by the sweetness of many flowers of the Holy Scriptures. "Qu'elle avait recueillé et transforme en un miel delicieux comme un abeille vigilante sous l'inspiration de Dieu, pour l'honneur du Christ et de son Église, aussi, les engageait elle à servir de ce miel comme un aliment de leur âme, afin qu'étant pénétrées des dèlices spirituelles, elles vècussent sur la terre en toute sècurite et arrivassent à jouir de l'èsternelle félicité."

Then followed many pious extracts on the Creator, the Angels; the Creation of the world and immortality. There were also curious notions regarding the principles of existence and divinity, interspersed with dissertations upon the garden and the culture of fields, land and sea, the winds, physical geography, the stars and the Zodiac. One curious decoration, entitled "Ludus Monstrorum," showed the figures of two men separated by a table, and holding in their hands the ends of two cords on which were suspended two small dolls, costumed as cavaliers and armed "cap à pie," who were made to perform by pulling the cords, something like those figures of marionettes, beloved by children. Under this picture was a lengthy allegory of Ulysses and the three Sirens, a study of the offices of the church, and a collection of precepts on the diverse states of society and the duties of the individual. Then followed a little verse against the practise of usury, a dissertation upon Anti-Christ, and a list of the Popes up to Clement III. Some calendars and ingenious chronological combinations ended the collection. But it was the naïve paintings and illuminations that lent most value to the great book, showing armor, architecture, costumes and furniture and such things in the greatest detail.

The Germans, vaunting ever their perfect "Kultur," did not hesitate to destroy this incomparable manuscript, together with thousands of other precious books contained in the Strassburg Library, even as they destroyed and burned the Library at Louvain in 1914.

Following the rue du Jeu-des-Enfants, one comes upon the most ancient building in Strassburg, the hoary old church of Pierre-le-Vieux, which is said to date from A. D. 60. Here are found some fine paintings of the Martin Schongauer school, and four bas-reliefs by the sculptor Wagner, which are most interesting. Continuing along the banks of the Ill, one passes the German garrison, ever an eyesore to the loyal Alsatians, and through the Allée de Robertsan reaches the promenade of Le Notre and the Orangerie, the most beautiful park in the city. The Jardin des Contades is no more; this charming place, where formerly the quaint "Kermis" was held annually; where the brightly painted booths of the marionettes were surrounded by spell-bound children, who watched with delight the trials of "Mère Michel," and "Geneviève de Brabant," is gone. Gone, too, is the celebrated restaurant Lips, where diners used to throw bread crusts down to a huge black bear in a sort of deep well. Gone is the large cage of storks, beloved of children. In its place is a huge ugly modern German building, looking entirely out of place, of course, and a standing example of the Teutonic lack of taste.

Of course one must make mention of what is perhaps the most characteristic feature of Strassburg, the storks. These large and curious-looking birds are the joy of the children, and the pride of the townspeople, who have a superstitious affection for them. The school children have a pretty little song, which they sing in the spring when they are looking for the appearance of the first comer. It runs:

> Ci-gogn, Ci-gogn, t'as d'la chance,
> Tous les ans tu pass's en France
> Ci-gogn, Ci-gogn, rapport nous,
> Dans ton bec un p'tit piou-piou!

First comes an old bird, who circles about the roof-tops, looking for a good place to begin the new nest, or to see if the old one is still where she left it in the first chill late autumn day. A pretty little girl informed me with an air of great gravity and confidence "that the storks came every year from Prussia; that they bore on their wings the Prussian colors, black and white, but that it was not their fault, it was in punishment for a *sin* which the first stork had committed—oh—*ages* and *ages* ago; that they had also very large mouths—'toute comme les Prussians,' and that they went away to find a warm place in the winter, but returned in the spring to count all the new babies that had arrived during their absence."

The people in the older parts of the town cast out on the roofs of the houses small bundles of faggots, which serve as foundations for the nests, and for days after their arrival the early morning hours are melodious with the whistling of the birds, busily preparing the great, shaggy nests. In olden times it was customary to greet the first arrivals by blowing a horn. Even now, the people believe that storks nesting on one's chimney-top bring good luck to all beneath that roof tree, and that no lightning will ever strike a house so protected. They say that should a stork alight on the street before a young girl and walk toward her, it is an unfailing sign of her early engagement in marriage. In upper Alsace the school boys sing a song something like this in the dialect:

> Storik, Storik, Langabein!
> Dra mi uf'm Buckel heim.
> Wohi—wohi?
> In's Alsace ni.

that is:

> Stork, Stork Longlegs,
> Take me home on your back—
> Where to?
> To Alsace.

As soon as the nest is finished, the birds take turns in sit-ing on the large eggs, and in a short time the scrawny young are hatched out. It is most amusing to watch the parent birds teaching the young to balance and fly, and later to steal any light object left within their reach. They seek their food on the banks of rivers and in marshy places, eating an astonishing number of frogs and mice, which they skillfully catch. M. Charles Grad, in his book, "Alsace," tells touchingly of seeing the return of the flock of storks to Strassburg in the month of March, 1871, when they flew distractedly over the ruins, vainly seeking their old nesting places, which were destroyed in the bombardment. There is a town ordinance which pro-tects them, but no law is necessary for their protection, so beloved are they. Even in the very oldest engravings of the town the bird is shown on the chimney tops of the quaint old timbered and dormered houses of the Market

Place, notably over the "Pfennigthurm," a high and square tower which stood at the angle of the "Barfusser-platz," now the Place Kleber.

Loyal Alsatians would not think of leaving Strassburg without going out to Kehl by tramway, to salute the statue of the brave Desaix, erected by Napoleon I to the hero of Marengo. On the east side is a tremendous new iron bridge over the river, each end of which is ornamented by most beautifully designed gateways, surmounted by artistic Gothic spires springing from open galleries. One cannot but contrast this beautiful bridge with those ugly towers over our own East River, and wonder why it is that we can not have structures embodying the artistic as well as the purely useful. Here formerly were very old bridges of boats across the river, which must have been very picturesque and archaic; but there is nothing archaic here now. Long lines of heavily-laden barges, with a forest of masts, are stretched along the busy quays, and in the distance is a heavy curtain of dark green poplars, behind which lies the land whose ruthless ruler dominates these fair lost Provinces of France.

The Real Reason

The Real Reason

IN a triangle of territory formed by the prolongation of the forest of Nonnenbrusch (le taillis des Moines), of which the base extends from Cernay to Mulhouse, where the point rests between the villages of Wittelsheim and Ensisheim, and at the confluence of the rivers Thur and l'Ill, lies the real reason of Germany's present refusal even to consider the restoration of the provinces to France.

This refusal has nothing to do with affection for the German inhabitants; or for the beauty of the great forests; or the ruins of the ancient strongholds and châteaux scattered over the region. And it certainly is not concerned with the lives of the devoted and patriotic French people who, in spite of the intolerable conditions imposed upon them by the usurper, cling so tenaciously to this fair land, conditions which have during the last forty-eight years brought them to the very verge of despair; conditions which I have hardly touched upon in this brief and fragmentary account of their lives and customs.

The real reason, apart from the military value of the mountain barrier so wonderfully fortified since the

315

ALSACE-LORRAINE

Franco-Prussian war, lies beneath the soil, so enriched by the blood of the French patriots.

Under this sacred soil lies a vast treasure house in which nature has stored a material which plays a tremendous part in the prosperity of nations. Not only are there rich mines of silver, copper, cobalt, arsenic, and iron, scattered over the region and in the valley of Sainte-Marie-aux-Mines, but there are here vast mines of potash, without which Germany cannot exist. I endeavored to obtain some facts regarding these potash mines, but my questions were evaded. Attempts which I made to turn conversations upon the subject were most skilfully blocked. Town officials whom I approached, while most affable and polite so long as I confined my questions to purely social matters, promptly became incommunicative when my inquiries touched upon matters connected with these mines. So I became even more curious regarding them. But beyond the following facts regarding their discovery and exploitation, I could gain nothing.

In the year 1879 one Gustav Dollfus, a citizen of Mulhouse who was engaged in mining experiments at Dornach, discovered traces of salt of potassium at a depth of one hundred yards. He promptly reported this discovery to his principals, but for some reason his report was pigeonholed and no action was taken upon it, as far as he could discover. Shortly afterwards he was appointed to a position requiring his removal to a distant town.

Apparently the vast wealth lay concealed until the year 1904, when M. Joseph Vogt, the head of the house of Vogt Brothers of Niederbruck in Upper Alsace, conceived the idea of exploring the locality for petroleum.

Under the researches of M. Vogt and two prominent engineers, Burcher and Griser, a great deposit of salt of potash was revealed at a depth of some six or seven hundred metres. After two years of experimenting and tentative borings, they formed a company with the aid of capitalists called the "Société Anceli," and sunk one hundred and thirty shafts in the territory. These being productive, they obtained the further concession of 19,000 hectares of land, which was immediately exploited with the result that at the beginning of the war (1914) the mines produced 800 tons daily.

Some time during the summer of 1914 the mines were quietly absorbed by a powerful Prussian company known as the "Deutsche Kaliverke." The mines were known under the names of "Marie"; "Max"; "Joseph"; "Elsa"; and "Marie Louise." These were united with three other groups comprising the "Winterschall," which includes the "Theodor"; the "Prince Eugene," near Wittenheim; the "Hohenzollern," and the great group known as the "Alsacien-Française," the latter founded for the exploitation of "Sainte-Thérèse," which includes the companies working the mines known as "Alex" and "Rudolf." The "Prince Eugene," near Wittenheim, comprises about 3,209 hectares of land, and produces salt of which 25 per cent. is chloride of potassium.

The "Alex" and "Rudolf" cover nearly, if not quite, 6,600 hectares of land, according to my informant. M. P. Sallior, writing in *La Nature*,[1] says that "In 1909, northeast of Mulhouse, a great deposit of potash was found. This mine was named 'Amélie' of Wittelsheim." The first shafts were crushed by "congélation." These shafts cost 2,500,000 francs and two years of work. The first cars filled with the potash were sent up from the mine in January, 1910, and the deposit was found to be of incredible richness. In 1912 the working force was increased to 200 miners and the daily extraction totaled 300 tons, each mine producing one and one half tons.

The potash veins are red and gray in color alternately, being a mixture of chlorate of potash and chlorate of sodium. The Reichweiler factory is equipped for the daily treatment of 260 tons of pure mineral, which produces from 40 to 50 tons of chlorate of potassium.

The "Amèlie" mine exploited to-day (1918) produces 9,000 tons of rough salt corresponding to fifteen wagons per diem. Increased facilities have resulted in an out-

[1] "La Nature," Deuxieme Semestre, 1917.

318

put of 800,000 tons per annum. The cost per ton to produce is fifteen francs, and the product is sold at the mine for thirty francs per ton. These then are some of the riches of Alsace-Lorraine upon which Germany has had a strangle hold for the last forty-eight years. What a rôle this territory will play when Germany is called upon to "pay up" after her defeat!

The Land of Tears

The Land of Tears

WHEN one speaks of Alsatians, one means by this designation those inhabitants born of parents whose ancestors have always been Alsatians, or more liberally, those whose parents were citizens of the Provinces of Alsace-Lorraine prior to the Franco-Prussian war. The settlers from Germany (called "immigres" by the people) and their descendants since that date are never really or openly recognized as Alsatians by the "ancients," as they style themselves, from whom by their nationality, their morality and habit of thought and manners, they are separated by an insurmountable barrier. Forced to daily commerce with the invaders, they limit it to the most formal intercourse; there can never be a common ground of intimacy between them, opposed as they are by both sentiment and feeling. This line of separation is marked by the absence of all social relations. They have separate clubs and circles, also marriages between the "immigres" and the Alsatians are very rare. They are frowned upon. An Alsatian girl who so far forgot her country and her people would be socially dead. Should it be necessary for an Alsatian to sit in public with the German officials at some ceremony, his private character or opinions are not thus sacrificed, but he does not for one moment permit intimacy of any sort from the officials. These seek in every way, one is told, to introduce and force themselves into the exclusive circles of the native born, but they rarely succeed. This state of affairs facilitates the solution of the present problem for the Alsatians, who are making ready to take once more their place as part of the French nation.

The Alsatians are French, body and soul. It will never be possible for Prussia to make them any other than French. The Alsatians hate the Germans. Any traveler, such as the writer, who merely passed through the Provinces, could plainly judge of the attitude of the people towards the invaders. It was impossible to mistake it. Of a population of nineteen hundred thousand inhabitants, the hated "immigres" number four hundred thousand, inclusive of the military, the German officials and their families. It will be seen then that Germany has left little undone in the last forty-seven years in the attempt to Teutonize the land.

Let us see, briefly, just how the Germans administer the affairs of these unfortunate and suffering people, against their will. The executive power is, of course, in the hands of the German Emperor. A "Statthalter" is appointed by him, with delegated powers, which he divides with a so-called chef de l'Administration, styled Minister of Alsace-Lorraine. All other Ministers, Secretaries of State, and under Secretaries and functionaries, down to well-nigh the smallest clerk, are named by the Emperor.

The Ministry of Alsace-Lorraine is divided into four offices as follows: Interior, Finances, Justice, Instruction, the latter under an official designated as "Oberschulrat."

The laws of Alsace-Lorraine are subject to the approbation of the Emperor, and are submitted to him by the Landesausschuss and the Bundesrat. There is a "Landtag," or Parliament, composed of two chambers. The first is that of the members of the right, who are those "elected," and those named and appointed by the Emperor. Five of these are the Bishops of Strassburg and Metz; the two presidents of the Protestant Cults; and the president of the Court of Appeals of Colmar. Eighteen members elected are as follows: a representative of the Israelite consistory, chosen from their own body; one from the University of Strassburg, elected by the professors of the University; four representatives of the towns of Strassburg, Mulhouse, Metz and Colmar, elected by the municipalities; four members elected by the Chambers of Commerce of these towns; six elected by the Council of Agriculture, of whom one is chosen from among the small proprietors; and the remaining two elected by the Chamber of Artisans of Alsace-Lorraine.

The Constitution apparently provides for a representative of the workmen, but this is said to be a farce. The Emperor has the right to name substitutes, and to reject any or all who are elected. Comment is unnecessary. The members are elected for five years. The Second Chamber is composed of sixty deputies elected by the electoral districts for five years, by secret ballot. These two chambers have the right to formulate and propose the passage of bills and laws, but these must have the sanction of the Emperor and the Prime Minister at Berlin before they can be passed! Comment again is unnecessary.

The "Statthalter," provided by Berlin, gives "instructions" to the delegates of Alsace-Lorraine, and it may be taken for granted that these "instructions" are entirely in accord with the views of the Prime Minister and the Emperor.

Those ancient laws of the second Empire, which were abrogated in France as being against the liberties which should obtain in a modern state, were revived and put in force by order of the Emperor. The most unpopular and unjust of these are maintained and constantly cited by the German officials to prove to the Alsatians that German laws are so much more enlightened and modern than those of France, and that "in time," these oppressive laws shall be repealed. To prove how Germany has continued to treat Alsace-Lorraine as a foreign territory: up to the year 1902 the Statthalter was directed "in case of danger to public security to use immediately all or any measures which he judged necessary." This was afterwards abrogated, but its spirit remains against all the pretended guarantees of civil rights under the adroitly-worded constitution. Let any question whatever concerning their rights be brought up for discussion, and the people are conclusively shown that they have no rights, save those designated as such by the Emperor. This is the situation at present (1918).

Germany has endeavored to confuse the world regarding Alsace-Lorraine, yet the matter is perfectly plain. Alsace-Lorraine always has and does still vehemently protest against the German yoke. Even Germany will not venture to assert that the provinces were taken from France with the consent of their inhabitants, and now, after forty eight years they are still protesting against the alien domination. The criminal acts of the Germans in the invaded territories during the last three years are a carrying out in a larger way of the indignities practised by them in Alsace-Lorraine. Louvain and Ypres and Malines are but aggrandisements of the Zabern affair.

Alsace-Lorraine has been the laboratory in which the

Germans have nurtured those noxious germs with which they are strewing Europe. In the "land of tears" the invaders have demonstrated the "doctrine of force and the gospel of terror as applied to a helpless people." Evidently they care nothing for the people, to whom they toss the dried crusts which constitute the so-called self-government accorded to the provinces in the "Chambres des Deputes d'Alsace-Lorraine." There can be no peace in Europe until both Belgium and Alsace-Lorraine are restored, the first to its rightful independence; the second to France. The principle at issue is the same with both.

Twice now Germany has thrust her blood-stained sword into the vitals of Europe, carving away each time greatly coveted cities and regions rich in minerals. Now the Teuton attempts to hold and control a great highway across Europe, including the rich potash and iron districts of Lorraine and the Belfort gate to Franche Comte. Germany and the Kaiser have in their minds the picture of a great Teutonic Empire surrounded by enslaved states obedient, mutilated and crushed to her will, yet contributing to her might, a dream that must not, shall not be realized.

Written in the soul of every loyal Alsatian in letters of blood against a background of fire, is the treaty of Frankfort, dated May 10, 1871. Article one reads as follows: "France renounces, in favor of the German Empire, all rights and titles to the territories situated east of the boundaries designated below. The German Empire shall possess these territories forever in full sovereignty and ownership."

This is the loot won in the Franco-Prussian war, Alsace-Lorraine. Professor Charles Downer Hazen, of Columbia College,[1] sums the matter up as follows: "No honest man believes that because Germany has controlled a tenth of France for the past three years she has the slightest right to that territory or ever will have, or ever could have. If she should keep her grip upon them for forty years and more, as she has kept it upon Alsace-Lorraine, she would have no greater right than on the first day of her unspeakable aggression. There is no more a question of Alsace-Lorraine to-day, after forty-eight years of occupation, than there is of the Department of the North after three years of occupation. If the German annexations of 1870 are justified, then the actual annexations of the present war are justified. The two cases stand upon an absolute parity. The people of Alsace-Lorraine have never admitted the right, they have only admitted the fact, of German rule, as no doubt the peasants of northern France have done and are perforce doing at the present moment.

"Ought there to be a referendum? No one would think of demanding that a popular vote should be taken in the Department of the North, for instance, to see if it

---

[1] "Alsace-Lorraine under German Rule," Charles Downer Hazen.

should become French again. There is no more reason for consulting Alsace-Lorraine, taken forty-six years ago, by precisely the same methods.

"If the proposition had actually been realized, made in 1917 by the German Secretary to the Mexican Government that, for services to be rendered to Germany by Mexico and Japan by their waging war upon the United States, Mexico should be rewarded by the acquisition of Texas, New Mexico and Arizona, does any sane person believe that the people of the United States, or the people of the States concerned, would, after forty years, have consented to submit the question of their return to the United States to a popular vote, conducted by the Mexican Government?

"The practical difficulties in the way of a referendum arise from the initial act of violence. Who would be the citizens of Alsace-Lorraine entitled to vote and to decide by their vote the fate of the Provinces? Should they be only the present residents? But over four hundred thousand Alsatians and Lorrainers have, owing to the annexation, left their country without hope of return, and have kept their love of it undimmed in the bitterness of exile, of poignant separation from friends and relatives. Are they and their sons, who have paid this heavy price for their fidelity to the fundamental principle in which every true American believes and must believe, because it is the very cornerstone of our national independence and freedom, are these people to have nothing to say at the time when the reunion of their provinces with France is among the possibilities, and are the Germanizing agents and immigrants in Alsace to have the vote in such a plebiscite? Again, who would conduct the referendum? In view of the ruthless regime of murder, imprisonment, espionage and delation which Germany installed in the provinces in August, 1914, would a referendum conducted under German authority be apt to be honest and scrupulous? This issue does not admit of compromise. It must be kept as clear cut as it is in its essential nature. The principle at the basis of the Treaty of Frankfort must be repudiated and emphatically discredited by its complete and resounding reversal. Never at any time has Alsace-Lorraine admitted that it was German. It declared the Treaty of Frankfort null and void, and it has never rescinded that declaration.

"The character of the German Government for forty-eight years, the very provisions of German legislation during all those years; the measures of the German administration; the occasional admissions of German officials as to the real situation, all show that the official affirmation that Alsace-Lorraine has become thoroughly German has not been believed even in the official circles which have made the affirmation. Their conduct has belied their words. Has German policy in Alsace-Lorraine at any time since 1870 been based upon the theory that a people who admittedly were opposed to annexation have become reconciled and are loyal Germans? What has Germany done to turn hatred into love, dissatisfaction into contentment?

"Friedrich Naumann has admitted in his recent book [1] that 'the modern Germans almost everywhere in the world are unfortunately bad Germanizers.' There is no more notorious commonplace in European politics than the egregious failure of the German to Germanize or even conciliate. Germany's Polish, Danish and French subjects are eloquent witnesses to this incapacity. Germany can hold people in subjection; she cannot or will not give them freedom.

"It has been suggested that Alsace-Lorraine be made an independent and autonomous monarchy with a royal house of its own within the German Empire. It also has been suggested that it be made an independent and naturalized state outside the German Empire as well as outside France. These are but ways of evading the problem, not ways of repairing a grievous wrong which has been and still is a serious public injury, an offense to the world's sense of justice, and a menace to the world's peace. They ignore the rights and wishes of the people concerned. The wrong can be repaired in only one way—by the return of these provinces to France, where they belong and where they desire to be."

[1] "Central Europe."

THE LAND OF TEARS

This is the beginning and end of the whole question.

We sat after dinner on a bench beneath a large tree in the hillside garden of the small but well kept inn, where we were to spend our last night in Alsace-Lorraine. Here we were joined by our opposite neighbor at the table d'hôte. "You permit, Madame and Monsieur?" He lighted his after dinner cigar and puffed away contentedly, putting his gaitered feet up on the low stone wall which separated the garden from the roadway. Before us lay the vast golden and green panorama of the French valley under the glow of a spectacular sunset. "Yes, Madame and Monsieur, as you say, you have now seen and known Alsace-Lorraine, as tourists, of course, it is well understood, but nevertheless, one can see that you have penetrated somewhat beneath the surface. But have you understood that 'l'âme n'y est plus'?—that since the annexation of our beloved land, our 'land of tears' is as the house of the dead? We are in mourning, Monsieur and Madame! In mourning for nearly fifty years! You English and Americans, M'sieu', do not perhaps appreciate what the word 'Patrie' means to a Frenchman, for you do not know what it means to have foreign soldiers occupying and ruling irresistibly your land and your home. You have not seen your fields trampled by the enemy's cavalry, or your fruit trees cut down and wantonly destroyed; your homes defiled and leveled to heaps of ashes. Thus you cannot imagine the sense of cruel wrong that we Frenchmen feel when our sacred soil is violated. Thus again perhaps you will not understand why our people here in Alsace-Lorraine cannot utter the word 'Patrie' with dry eyes."

Here in the Vosges actual twilight, with its deep glow, has longer life, and a more prolonged color than when seen from the valley level. Overhead the reds and saffrons of the sunset were of an astonishing richness of color, and the whole countryside was bathed in crimson and gold with deep violet shadows. The small town awkwardly climbing the hill at each side of the steep road, took on new splendors of gilding; the tree tops shone ruddily; the old church tower was set in a prismatic frame work, its cross all golden against the green, and in the tower finials the rooks circled as the color softened and deepened. Over the valley in France the shadows lengthened in tones of saffron and lapis lazuli. Our loquacious companion had relapsed into silence. The great hills of the Vosges threw their shadows over the French valley—here and there jagged rocks, the gray towers of a distant cathedral; long winding roadways like violet ribbons across the dim landscape; a river bed here and there with an embowered mill, and crooked lanes emerging and vanishing into the dusk.

The next day it rained. Autumn drew aside her scarlet and gold draperies, and the stage was set for winter. Enormous storms of hail and sleet rolled down the mountains and spread themselves over the valleys, while on the peaks above the black clouds split themselves in fury. In the midst of one of these storms we left Alsace-Lorraine.

Bibliography

Ardouin-Dumazet, Voyage en France, 48° Serie, Les Provinces Perdues, La Haute-Alsace, Paris-Nancy, Berger-Levrault, in 8°,
1907.

Daniel Blumenthal, "L'Alsace Lorraine."

Henri Welschinger (Membre de l'Institut), "Moeurs et Costumes."

Ralph Adams Cram, "The Heart of Europe."   Scribner, 1915.

Emile Hinzelin, Director "La France de Demain."

Le Roy de Sainte-Croix, Les anniversaires Glorieux de l'Alsace,
Paris-Strasbourg, 1881.

Histoire documentaire de l'Industrie de Mulhouse et de ses environs au XIX° siècle (Publication de la Société Industrielle
de Mulhouse), Mulhouse, Bader, 2 Vols. in folio, 1902.

L. M. Mulhouse; Revue de Paris, 15 Mars 1898.

Aug. Lalance, Mulhouse Français, Paris, Chaix, in 8°, 1912; Ch.
Grad, L'Alsace, Paris, Hachette, in folio, 1885.

Charles Downer Hazen, Alsace-Lorraine Under German Rule.
Henry Holt & Co., N. Y.

Monstrelet, Chronicles.

Maurice Barrès, Les Provinces Captives.   Paris, Toulouse.

George Delahache, La Cathedral de Strasbourg.   Paris, Longuet
Edit.

Index

INDEX

338

INDEX

INDEX

INDEX

INDEX

INDEX

INDEX

36342712R00193

Made in the USA
Middletown, DE
31 October 2016